ENCOUNTERING
WORLD
RELIGIONS

ENCOUNTERING
WORLD
RELIGIONS

QUESTIONS OF RELIGIOUS TRUTH

GEOFFREY PARRINDER

CROSSROAD • NEW YORK

1987

The Crossroad Publishing Company,
370 Lexington Avenue, New York, N.Y. 10017

First published in 1987 by T. & T. Clark Ltd., Edinburgh, Scotland.

——Printed in the United Kingdom.

Library of Congress Cataloging in Publication Data
Parrinder, Edward Geoffrey.
Encountering world religions.
Includes index.
1. Religions.   2. Parrinder, Edward Geoffrey.
I. Title.
BL80.2.P345   1987   291   86–29385
ISBN 0–8245–0826–2

CONTENTS

CONTENTS

Chapter One

AND IS IT TRUE?

In his *Cautionary Verses* Hilaire Belloc, 'Upon being asked by a Reader whether the verses contained in this book were true', wrote:

> And is it True? It is not True,
> And if it were it wouldn't do,
> For people such as me and you.

That was fine for cautionary tales, but a similar question is often raised about the religions of the world, or other religions than our own. Are they true, or our own true and all the others false?

The existence of many religions in the world, and the knowledge of their teachings and practices that is now available, present challenges and problems. Even in the academic study of what is called 'comparative religion' questions of truth are complex. Is such a study only concerned with fallacies, an interest in the untrue? Or does it try to show that religions are true in principle, either that all are true equally or some more than others? It would hardly be admitted that schools and colleges where there are such courses are not concerned with truth, yet to establish the truth or falsehood of particular religions is difficult on general principles.

From inside a religion a believer may make a dogmatic claim that his own religion is true, and Christians do this in reciting creeds, but there are equally confident declarations in other religions. The Muslim assertion that the Koran is the Word of God, the Hindu intuition that Thou art Brahman, the Buddhist belief that Gautama is the God beyond the gods, are all uncompromising claims. We are faced not only with devotional practices and teachings, but with assumptions of truth and authority.

'And is it true?' is a personal question, raised by the demands of the religion into which one is born. It is also a social question, both for religious communities and for political states which contain or encounter religious organizations. The challenges of politics, economics, technology and science all have some bearing upon religion. If Christianity and Judaism in the West have faced these challenges to some extent in the last century, their impact is now being felt everywhere. Buddhism in China has been persecuted as Christianity has in Russia. Religious revivals or reactions, for example in Iran, bring their own problems.

Some of the largest religions, and some smaller ones, are missionary. They believe in the universal validity of their faith and intend to communicate it to other people. They have world-ambitions: the Kingdom of God on earth, the House of Islam, the one sole Buddha-vehicle. They encounter the world-claims of Communism or Capitalism, of state-direction or democracy. Their missionaries have been admired by supporters and criticized by opponents, not always unjustly. But is there still a Christian mission? Or for that matter a Buddhist, an Islamic or a Hindu? And what kind of mission? Should it require converts to abandon all their own inherited faith, make a complete renunciation? If not, would the result be syncretism, a mixture, or plain infidelity?

There are many questions, and the answers may not be easily found, at least in one generation. Meanwhile we live in a world that is not only multi-racial but multi-religious. Asian religions are no longer confined to lands east of Suez, and Christianity exists in most countries of the world. In newspapers and on television screens all of us may see the most diverse religious practices.

This book is an attempt to show the impact of different

religions upon each other, or upon one person after sixty years of study and encounter. Since most readers will probably have the background of the Christian tradition, the problems of that tradition are especially considered. Apologies are made for occasional use of the personal pronoun, but perhaps parts of autobiography may show some of the pleasures and problems of religious encounter. These are some adventures among religions, a kind of pilgrimage of faith, from a restricted beginning to contact with many varieties of religious experience.

A start is made with Buddhism, because some of my earliest and latest experiences were with this great Asian faith. From there short chapters consider in turn some aspects of and problems of encounter with Shinto, Hinduism, Sikhism, Islam, Judaism, Africa and fringe religions, proceeding to questions on missions, teaching and dialogue.

This book is a series of sketches of some aspects of the religions of the modern world. Countless studies have been made of all the religions, and here elements have been chosen which have touched my own experiences, so that there is a personal as well as a factual statement. This is a search for truth, which is not ended, and light is welcomed from whatever quarter it may come.

Light is a useful example, for it is made up of different colours, and the spiritual life of mankind is similarly diverse. Artists and wise men have seen this and have sometimes expressed their feelings in comparable terms. In the early nineteenth century the poet Shelley wrote in *Adonais:*

> The One remains, the many change and pass;
> Heaven's light forever shines, Earth's shadows fly;
> Life, like a dome of many-coloured glass
> Stains the white radiance of Eternity.

Over two thousand years earlier an Indian sage declared in the Upanishads:

> The One who is himself without colour
> by the manifold exercise of his power
> distributes many colours in his hidden purpose,
> into whom in the beginning and the end
> the whole universe dissolves—
> He is God!
> May he grant us a clear understanding.

Chapter 2

EARNEST HUNT FOR BUDDHA

English Buddhist Priest
Before the first World War a young Englishman, Ernest Hunt, went abroad on business. He had always been interested in religion, brought up in the Church of England he soon ventured into Methodism, the Salvation Army, Roman Catholicism and beyond. In Hawaii he fell ill and was cared for by a Buddhist family, then he married the daughter and became a Buddhist. Now he had a faith and a community and tried to help it.

Hawaii has a large Buddhist population from Japan but the children who went to mission schools were subjected to Christian teaching. After the death of his first wife Ernest Hunt began Buddhist classes for Japanese children and with his second wife, an English Quaker lady, they obtained governmental recognition for Buddhist schools which have developed ever since. Ernest was ordained a Buddhist priest with the name of Shinkaku, 'new word'. Buddhist priests in the northern Mahayana tradition are often married, celibacy being reserved for monks and nuns. Ernest and Dorothy had a number of children, but left them freedom to choose their own religion and none of them became Buddhists.

Back in England Ernest Hunt's parents were shocked when he became a Buddhist and a priest. Was not this a betrayal of Christianity? Yet they had supported missions for conversion of Buddhists, which would have involved abandonment of Buddhist family religion. When Ernest paid a short visit home, his family thought he would have to observe food taboos or demand only vegetarian meals. But he ate anything, since the Buddhist prohibition was not strictly against eating meat but against taking life oneself.

Ernest Hunt's two sisters absorbed Buddhism into their Christianity, and since both had already been interested in Theosophy it was not difficult to extend their sympathies. This was where the Buddha slipped quietly over my horizon, for Katie Hunt was ill and came to live with us after being told that she could not survive six months. She stayed thirty years and became a close friend, bringing stories of Ernest and books on Buddhism that aroused new interests. In particular there was a Life of the Buddha which had attractive pictures and opened a different world of ideas.

We did not meet Ernest Hunt till years later but he wrote occasionally and engaged in a sort of religious dialogue. Canon B. H. Streeter had written a book on *The Buddha and the Christ* and Ernest was asked to give his opinion of it. He thought the book was too critical, in studying Buddhism from the outside and making points which a Buddhist would not admit. As in much inter-religious argument, the Canon seemed to be talking to himself and little aware of the feelings of people who practised the religion.

In 1964 my wife and I visited the Hunts in Honolulu on our way to Australia, when Ernest was an old man and he died not long after. He was a priest at a Soto Zen temple, a splendid and colourful building, with images and hangings, incense and lights. Ernest was still very English, patriotic, and amused and pleased that with the entry of Hawaii into the United States the Union Jack, as part of the flag of Hawaii, would return into the American colours.

Zen and Pure Land
Ernest Hunt had helped to establish both Soto Zen and Shin-Shu temples in Honolulu, and in conversations he expounded some of their teachings and practices. Zen is the Japanese version of the Chinese Ch'an school of Buddhism, which took its name from the Indian *dhyana*, meaning 'meditation'. All forms of

Buddhism teach meditation, though not everybody practises it, but Zen has tended to emphasize meditation before scripture study. Yet there are scriptural passages which Zen disciples constantly repeat, such as the twenty-fifth chapter of the Lotus scripture. In Japan this is called the Kannon or Kwannon Sutra, because of its praise of the great Buddhist saviour Kwannon, the Chinese lady Kwanyin.

Zen Buddhism teaches that 'enlightenment' (satori) may come suddenly in a flash of awareness. To help their pupils achieve this state some Zen teachers recommend the use of Koans, nonsense problems, such as 'what is the sound of one hand clapping?' Because enlightenment can come at any time, Zen can be practised in daily life and many of the arts have been inspired by it: painting, calligraphy, gardening, flower arrangement, and even archery and swordsmanship. This explains part of the appeal of Zen to the West, and to the Japanese military classes, as it seems to be a workaday no-nonsense religion. Perhaps it also attracts the indolent, if enlightenment can come without doing anything, though in its home countries Zen is a strict discipline of mind and body and Zen monks endure severe training.

Ernest Hunt referred to the writings of the Japanese scholar D. T. Suzuki, who for many years made Zen known to the western world by numerous books. But Suzuki gave the teaching of the smaller Rinzai school of Zen, named after its ninth century founder. Most Japanese Zen believers, and Ernest Hunt himself, followed the Soto school which was named after a Chinese patriarch and introduced into Japan in the twelfth century. Soto relies on meditation and does not favour the problems and questions of Rinzai. In Honolulu the Soto Zen are well organized and they have Sunday Schools, public services, meditation groups, women's societies and Young Men's Buddhist Associations.

Shin-Shu or Jodo, 'Pure Land', which Ernest Hunt also

helped to establish in Hawaii, is the Japanese form of Pure Land Buddhism, created or reinforced in Japan from the twelfth century and becoming the most popular of all Chinese and Japanese forms of Buddhism. Pure Land teaches faith in Amida, a legendary Buddha who dwells in the Pure Land or Western Paradise, a place not unlike the Shangri La of James Hilton's *Lost Horizon*. The Pure Land school teaches salvation by simple faith in Amida and repetition of his name is held to ensure entry into paradise. It was this doctrine of salvation by faith alone that alarmed the Jesuit missionaries in the sixteenth century. They went to Japan to leave behind such a heresy in Europe, and on meeting Pure Land they exclaimed, 'this is Lutheranism!'

Simple Scriptures?
Although Zen claims to sit lightly to the scriptures, Ernest Hunt and other Buddhist authorities recommended the reading of Buddhist texts in order to learn about the teachings of the religion. But this was not easy, although sometimes Buddhism is claimed to be a simple religion, or even just a morality. It is a modern fallacy that religious books are, or ought to be, easy reading, the kind of books that he who runs may read without stopping. The fact is that most scriptures are difficult, and there is wry truth in a verse in the Indian Upanishads which says that 'the gods love the cryptic and dislike the obvious'.

An introduction to eastern religions may come through reading an isolated verse from the scriptures, which strikes one as profound or illuminating, yet the texts in full are often difficult and obscure. Young and old buy selections from these scriptures which are published in great numbers, then they struggle with them and perhaps quote complex verses as plain and eternal truth. People who might scorn to read the Bible as old-fashioned, wrestle with books that for obscurity leave the Christian scriptures far behind. And even platitudes that might be despised in a western context may be revered if they come from the 'mystic East'.

Some people seek for the occult and esoteric within Buddhism, and may be puzzled with inscrutable verses or bewildered by impossible stories. In 1956 a so-called Dr Lobsang Rampa published a book, through Secker and Warburg, entitled *The Third Eye*. This claimed to be the autobiography of a Tibetan Lama, with his upbringing, the opening of a third eye in his forehead, his life as a Lama, a Buddhist abbot, and with details of Tibetan life such as the supposed invention of flying machines long before they were known in the West.

This book, and successors such as *Doctor from Lhasa*, reached a large market of those eager for secrets of the occult East. Although the author declared in his first words, 'I am a Tibetan', the publisher began to have doubts about the accuracy of the narratives. In a letter to *The Times Literary Supplement* in 1959 Fredric Warburg admitted that the author's real name was Cyril Henry Hoskins, a Devonshire plumber. Mr Warburg suggested, perhaps with tongue in cheek, that 'the mind boggles at the idea of two authors in one body struggling with each other to write his own book and choose his own publisher'. Subsequent books have come from other publishers but they have had a wide sale.

A great authority on Buddhist scriptures, Dr Edward Conze, has written caustically on the craving for even more esoteric Buddhist texts, saying that 'an interminable literature is addressed to a credulous public which expects to buy these secrets for a few shillings in a bookshop'. This applies particularly to Buddhist Tantra or 'mystery religions'. Most of these texts are magical, 'their rational content is negligible', they have slight literary merit and are written in a language that is little understood today. In so far as these works are secret they are in a code which nobody has broken, and if the translators claim to have received secret knowledge from 'occult masters', which they are now making public, then they are betraying their trust and are unworthy of attention.

Such Buddhist Mysteries may have been parallel to the Mysteries of ancient Greece, which were secret and therefore remain largely unknown. Or perhaps they were like those of Egypt, 'which turn out never to have existed'. But ignorance of their secrets does not stop would-be translators from complaining that the few texts available are 'all too brief', or accusing rival translators of 'scientific nonsense' or making 'totally false assumptions'.[1]

With Buddhism, as with other religions, the outsider needs to keep to simple and central texts. One may begin with the short Dhammapada, the 'Virtue-path', in some four hundred verses, which many Buddhists know by heart. This gives central Buddhist moral teachings, but they are abstract and hardly show Buddhism as a religion.

Later one may proceed to study portions of the canon of scripture of the Theravada (or Hinayana) Buddhists, as translated in numerous volumes by the Pali Text Society. The first part is the Vinaya Pitaka, 'Discipline Basket', full of rules for the monastic orders. This has been translated into English in five volumes but it is detailed, complex, and rarely read in English. The translator, a spinster, often put asterisks for certain passages, though from erotic verses that remain it seems that the monks had renounced the world but they could not get away from their imaginations, and they had 'the fascination of their repressions'. The Vinaya is hardly recommended for general reading, and the last part of the canon is equally difficult. This is the Abhidhamma' 'higher Dhamma' or meta-physics, which includes abstruse philosophical speculations.

It is the central body of scripture, the Sutta Pitaka, 'verse

[1] *Buddhist Thought in India*, 1962, p. 271f.

basket', which is most important for Buddhist and other readers. Even this is very long and complex, opening with the Net of Brahman or Perfect Net, which discusses sixty-two heretical forms of speculation about the world and the self. This is only one of hundreds of dialogues and stories, and most Buddhists know only selections, as in other religions the ordinary layman selects favourite passages and there are abbreviated versions of central teachings.

According to tradition the Indian prince Siddhartha Gautama, in the sixth century B.C., became discontented with an easy life, renounced his family and home, and wandered about for years seeking enlightenment. When this came he was a Buddha, an 'Enlightened One', and he proceeded to Sarnath near Benares to expound his convictions. His first sermon taught the Middle Way, between the extremes of sensuality and asceticism. It comprised four Noble Truths and the Noble Eightfold Path. The truths were of pain or suffering, the fact, the cause in desire and craving, the cessation in forsaking desire, and the way to it by the Path. The Noble (aryan) Eightfold Path begins with right views and intention, then practical right speech, action and livelihood, and ending with mental practice in right effort, mindfulness and concentration. This was to be the way for his disciples, leading to calm, insight and enlightenment.

In a second sermon on the Marks of Non-Self or Soul, the Buddha declared that the soul or self should not be identified with the five elements of the human person: body, feelings, perception, impressions or consciousness. He did not say here, as is sometimes assumed, that there is no soul, but that it cannot be grasped or apprehended. Similarly, he criticized those who speculated about the state of the soul after death, whether it is formed or formless, happy or miserable, finite or infinite. He taught Nirvana, 'blowing out', extinction of desires, as the goal of all endeavour and he emphasized the practical way of self-denial to bring deliverance from the troubles of this world. But what is the role of the Buddha himself, and is Buddhism a religion?

Is Buddhism a Religion?

The forms of Buddhism that have chiefly appealed to the West have either been the ethical teachings, or meditation and Zen. The moral precepts were some of the first to be translated into European languages in the nineteenth century, and to many scholars Buddhism seemed to be an ideally rationalistic religion, without the notions of God and the soul which dominated other religions. It was emphasized that the Buddha was a man, almost a 'mere' man, who taught self-salvation, if indeed there was a self to be saved. But on the ground, as visits to Buddhist countries show, matters are very different. Whether the Buddha taught religion or not, it is present in a big way, in one of the most widespread and ancient religions, in positive forms of worship.

When he went to Burma, says the American anthropologist Melford Spiro, it was in the hope of facing a 'stunning problem' and a great opportunity. For he had been told that Buddhism was an atheistic religion, rejecting belief in a soul, teaching that all life was suffering, and regarding salvation as extinction. But on arrival in the country, 'the problem turned out to be a pseudo-problem'. Some of these ideas were not normal Buddhism, some were distorted, and others were unknown to the faithful or ignored by them. He concluded that Buddhists and their religion 'differ very little from people and religions in general'.[2]

Buddhism in every land of its practice has the marks of a living religion, as I have remarked in visiting temples, shrines and monasteries in Sri Lanka, Burma, Hawaii, Hong Kong and

[2] *Buddhism and Society*, 1971, p. 10f.

Japan. I went to famous Buddhist remains in India at Ellora, Ajanta, Sanchi, Sarnath, Buddh-Gaya and other places where there are monuments, buildings and caves covered in sculptures of figures from Buddhist story. Here is all the social panorama from animals to warriors, and from naked girls to monks, and amid them all sits the Buddha in peace and compassion. At Gaya on the middle Ganges, where he was enlightened, the site is marked by a tall pyramidal temple lit to a golden brown by the sun. At Sarnath his first sermon is commemorated by a great stone tower, or stupa, which dates back to the Buddhist emperor Ashoka in 250 B.C. The sermon took place in a Deer Park, and for the celebration of the 2,500th anniversary in 1956 the Indian government restored part of the park, introduced some deer, and provided canteens for visitors and a Kiddies' Corner for children.

But is the Buddha himself a god, or is there no god? Basic Buddhist scriptures refer to a Hindu creator god, Brahma, who appears in both Hindu and Buddhist myths. But he is inferior to the Buddha himself, as all gods are, since they are still caught up in the round of birth, death and rebirth. There are plenty of gods in Buddhist stories, but they are lay figures around the central actor, the Buddha himself. He is the 'teacher of gods and men', 'the God above the gods', the saviour of those who go to him for refuge. At his enlightenment, he knew all things and beings past, present and future, with the omniscience of a super-deity. In worship the Buddha is the supreme being, a god in function, the great object of worship.

'The cognitive position', says the Sanskrit professor Richard Gombrich in a study of Buddhist practice in Sri Lanka, is that the Buddha was human, though the best of men, born into a noble family and caste and attaining the highest goal. But while 'cognitively human' he is 'effectively divine', since he has long since been deified by a 'personality cult'. The bridge from veneration of a teacher to worship as divine was the cult of

13

relics, and then temples and images of the Buddha reinforced the approximation to Hindu worship. Images are given offerings of food, since they incorporate a living presence which is dramatically revealed when the eyes are painted on the image. This 'eye festival' is so dangerous that the special craftsmen who perform it work in secret and use a mirror so as not to look at the image and eyes directly. When it is finished, the Buddha is prayed to for forgiveness and his living presence is believed to inform all worship and daily life.[3]

Many Buddhas

The Buddha is central in the lands of southern Asia which follow the Theravada, 'the doctrine of the elders', called by northern Buddhists Hinayana, 'lesser vehicle' as contrasted with their own Mahayana, 'great vehicle' of salvation for all beings. In Theravada one of the oldest and most repeated Buddhist cries of devotion claims: 'I go to the Buddha for refuge, I go to the Doctrine (*dhamma*) for refuge, I go to the Order of monks (*sangha*) for refuge'. The Buddha is first, and he gave the Doctrine and founded the Order. This refuge-formula is like liturgical statements in Hindu devotion, where the worshipper goes to Krishna or other gods for refuge.

In southern Theravada Buddhism there are other Buddhas, past and to come, in theory. But popular writings discuss the problems whether there can be two Buddhas at once and conclude that it is not possible. Firstly, because the world would not be able to support the weight of two Buddhas at once but would sink into the primeval ocean. Secondly, in view of the weaknesses of human nature, because if there were two Buddhas at once their followers would disagree, saying 'Your Buddha, our Buddha'. Two Buddhas at once would falsify the confessions that the Buddha is the foremost, the eldest, the best,

---

[3] *Precept and Practice*, 1971, pp. 81, 138ff.

the eminent, without a counterpart, and unrivalled. So there is only one Buddha for this present world era, and since it may last hundreds of thousands of years there is only one Buddha to concern us. In effect Theravada Buddhism sets out to be a faith in one God, a monotheism, except that it is no compliment to call the Buddha a god since he is far above them all, 'the God beyond the gods'.

In northern Buddhism, however, in China, Tibet, Korea, Japan and Vietnam, there are countless Buddhas and Bodhisattvas, 'beings of enlightenment'. It looks like polytheism, worship of many gods, though as so often in human affairs there is apparent inconsistency and people can worship one deity or many by turns, as worshippers of One God may revere saints and ancestors. It was this lush and complex Mahayana, 'great vehicle', Buddhism which attracted Ernest Hunt, with its wealth of religion and art in addition to its meditation and morality.

Among the highlights of a recent long stay in Japan were visits to Kamakura. Here the focus of devotion is a huge bronze statue, the Great Buddha (Daibutsu), which is not the historical Gautama of India but the mythical Amida Buddha of the Western Paradise. For over seven hundred years Amida has sat here among trees and green hills, a statue forty-three feet high and weighing nearly a hundred tons, one of the greatest bronzes in the world. Once sheltered by a tall building which was destroyed by a typhoon in the seventeenth century, Amida sits in the open air in endless meditation. It is a moving experience to gaze at this beautiful and simple figure, and Kipling's verses from two chapter headings of *Kim* spring to mind:

> Oh ye who tread the Narrow Way
> By Tophet-flare to Judgment Day,
> Be gentle when the heathen pray
> To Buddha at Kamakura!

> For whoso will, from Pride released,
> Contemning neither man nor beast,
> May hear the Soul of all the East
> Around him at Kamakura.

The local 'heathen' seemed intent on taking photographs of family groups, parties of schoolgirls asking to be snapped with strangers, and foreigners buying souvenirs. 'Wretched perfectionists', as the guide book calls them, have spoilt the view with a gateway in front and a concrete gallery behind the great figure. Yet people do pray at Kamakura, the usual temple tank provides water for ritual washing, and then the devout proceed to place flowers in front of the statue and bow to it with joined hands.

'The Soul of all the East' may be perceived in the prayers and devotions which struggle for expression among crowds of tourists. There is a remarkable universality in the simplicity of the overshadowing monument, which seems more impressive than an even larger bronze statue of Buddha Roshana at Nara. Amida Buddha meditates, with hands outspread and thumbs joined, not sleeping but abstracted, looking at and through the crowds. The figure expresses the appeal and a paradox of Buddhism.

The appeal is in the control, beyond self, the peace that comes by renouncing desire and the world itself. This is world-denial and there may seem to be disdain in the curling lips of the Amida statue. The paradox is that this world-denying monkish ideal developed into one of the great missionary religions of the world, whose envoys went as far as Egypt in the west, and now to America, and to Japan in the east. In this religion all the cares of daily life, its hopes and fears, worries and disasters, have been taken to the Buddha or Buddhas when men and women have gone to them for refuge.

Zen, forms of yoga, mystical and sexual Tantra, meditation,

prayer, devotion, world-denial and missionary enterprise, all have come from Buddhism. There is simple morality for daily life, compassion for all beings, and an ethereal philosophy which seeks to realize the Void or Nothingness. It is a 'catholic' selection, and it gives rise to new communal and pastoral movements, as we shall see.

Chapter Three

BUDDHIST NEW RELIGIONS

Praise of Nichiren

Arthur Koestler, after a brief visit to Japan, wrote that 'religious feeling is deader in Japan, and has been dead for a longer time, than in any of the great existing civilizations'.[1] He seems to have spent most of his time in discussion with Zen teachers, trying to make them admit that Nazism was not only foolish but evil, and assessing the contradictions in Japanese life symbolized as 'the Lotus and the Robot'. There is no indication that Koestler met with any of the so-called 'new religions' of Japan, whose followers are estimated at over thirty million and whose activities are widespread and profound.

In 1977 my wife and I were fortunate in being able to attend a great festival of one of the most lively religious organizations, visit its sacred buildings, and have the guidance of some outstanding scholars of modern Japanese life.

Rissho Koseikai, 'the Society for Establishment of Righteousness and Achievement of Fellowship', was founded in Tokyo in 1938 and now claims over four million members. Like some other new Buddhist sects in Japan it looks back to the Japanese reformer Nichiren of the thirteenth century. In October it holds as O-eshiki, a 'memorial service', for Nichiren which is one of the most colourful festivals.

In the heart of the western suburbs of Tokyo, from six o'clock in the evening great processions, with symbols and decorations, wound through the streets towards the massive temple buildings. The atmosphere was like a carnival, with massed spectators, costumed performers and decorated floats.

[1] *The Lotus and the Robot*, 1960, p. 268.

In each group a young woman marched first carrying the name of the ward in Chinese characters on a placard. Usually she was in western dress, wearing white gloves and walking intent and firmly. She was followed by a group of young men in shorts and shirts crossed with strips of cloth, dancing and jumping round a *mando* (a symbol, perhaps from the Indian *mandala*, a circle or symbolical diagram). This *mando* was generally a brass triangle or square at the end of a pole, fringed with cloth, and it was twirled round and raised aloft as the youths marched and danced.

Then came bands of men and women in uniform dress, mostly Japanese but some western, beating drums and metal bowls, or playing flutes. Many of them sang at the same time to a constant beat the Japanese version of the northern Buddhist common verse, 'Hail to the Jewel in the Lotus', sounding in the drumbeat as 'dondon dondoko dondon'. These musicians were followed by decorated and illuminated model pagodas on floats pulled by men or moved by a car engine. The pagodas bore brightly lit and coloured pictures of Buddhas and other heavenly beings, and above them waved wires of paper flowers bouncing around like baskets of Christmas decorations.

Group after group they came in orderly procession for over three hours, marching slowly, dancing, jumping, playing and singing. The watching crowds clapped each ward group as it passed, and hummed the ever-repeated verse till it became mechanical and soporific. The groups proceeded along the closed streets up to two great temples and mustered in the courtyards until they were finally dispersed. It was a long but always lively, colourful and impressive ceremony. The crowds of young men and women, chanting in praise of their founder and faith, had clearly spent a great deal of time, money and energy in preparing their different contributions, and this religion at least was not dead.

The main temple of Rissho Koseikai is the Great Sacred Hall, of overwhelming size and of mixed traditional and modern styles. The outside is covered with pink tiles and crowned with pure gold pinnacles. Inside there are red marble walls and staircases, with high-vaulted aluminium ceilings. It is immaculate, cleaned by constant bodies of volunteer workers. The Hall is centrally heated in winter and air-conditioned in summer, with an excellent cafeteria which provides cheap food in Japanese style, though members are allowed to bring their own provisions and buy only drinks.

At the festival, and while the processions were winding through the streets, meals were served in the hall and free food was offered to visitors. Tables were laid with many kinds of western and Japanese delicacies, there were self-service counters, and beer and saké wine were constantly brought by waitresses in uniform. It was natural to wonder what the teetotal Buddha would have thought of it, though similar speculations come at times about the founders of other religions, if they saw some activities of their followers today.

New Religions?
Rissho Koseikai is not the largest or most recent of Japanese 'new religions', though it has been closely studied by foreign scholars and more will be said of other important features in its life. Like some other movements, it is a development of Nichiren Buddhism, which is the most distinctively Japanese form of Buddhism. Pure Land faith religion is the most popular, but it came from China as did Zen.

Nichiren was a Japanese Buddhist monk who lived in the thirteenth century (1222–1282). His name meant 'sun-lotus', combining Shinto and Buddhist ideals, and he taught absolute devotion to the Lotus Sutra, the distinctive Mahayana scripture. Nichiren attacked other forms of Buddhism as heretical or failures and made outspoken criticism of rulers who had patronized them. He reserved special attacks for the Pure Land worshippers of Amida whose prayers, he said, instead of saving them would lead straight to hell. He urged his followers to action by imitating the northern Buddhist ideal of self-sacrifice for the good of others. He was persecuted himself and even condemned to death at Kamakura but saved, it is said, by miraculous intervention. Nichiren's example of aggressive activity and suffering, combined with a simplified faith, has made a lasting appeal to many Japanese, though there has been conflict with other forms of Buddhism.

Rissho Koseikai was founded in Tokyo in 1938 by Nikkyo Niwano and Mrs Myoko Naganuma, the first as organizer and the second as spiritual leader. They were devoted to the Lotus Sutra as taught by followers of Nichiren whose work had had a revival from the nineteenth century. Rissho Koseikai is a lay movement, without monks or priests, and its special concern with social reform was recognized in 1979 when Mr Niwano was awarded the prestigious Templeton Prize in that year for 'Progress in Religion', one of the few non-Christian recipients of the prize.

Even more successful than Rissho Koseikai in gaining popularity in Japan in modern times has been the aggressive Soka Gakkai, first registered as a 'new religion' in 1952 and now claiming fifteen million adherents. Its astonishing growth was linked with political power, and also at one time one out of every seven Japanese college students was claimed as a member. My colleague Noah Brannen in Tokyo made a study of Soka Gakkai some years ago with the sub-title 'Japan's Militant Buddhists'.

In the tradition of Nichiren, Soka Gakkai has used forceful tactics of mass-conversion by campaigns confessedly 'to exterminate all false religion' and help everybody 'achieve happiness now'. The name Soka Gakkai means 'Society for the Creation of Value'. Differently from most modern religious movements this sect has had a strongly nationalistic political arm. This is the Komeito, 'Clean Government Party', which appealed to lower middle class workers who felt caught between the capitalism of the ruling Liberal Democrats in Japan and the labour unions of the Socialists. In recent years, since Dr Brannen's study was made, Komeito has moved in varying directions. It made an agreement of mutual respect with the Communist Party, but when that lost heavily in elections it drew away again. It was difficult to see what policies Komeito would follow if it ever came to power, though its pugnacity seems to express some of the traditional Japanese militarism in other forms.

Rissho Koseikai, like most new religious organizations, has not formed a political party but prefers to form friendships with political figures and to exercise influence indirectly through dialogue and through the votes of its members. Soka Gakkai also has now declared that religion and politics are separate, and renounced former slogans like 'Buddhist democracy' and 'the unity of politics with Buddhist law'. In theory, it has reverted to being a purely religious movement though at elections people will probably vote for Komeito or whatever candidates are recommended to them. Tradition and hierarchy are so strong that although everyone is free to vote, the vote may be as the family, party or religion command.

There are other modern religious movements in Japan, and some have been described as 'thirteen sects of Shinto'. But the distinction between the traditional religion of Shinto and Buddhism which came from India via Korea and China, although convenient for study, is hard to maintain when practice is considered. There is much religious practice which is similar in the two traditions, and worshippers may hardly be aware whether the being they are addressing is a Shinto spirit or a Buddhist 'being of enlightenment'.

The largest of the 'Shinto sects' is Tenri-kyo, the 'Religion of Heavenly Wisdom', founded in 1838 by a woman, Miki

Nakayama. It now claims two million followers, has ten thousand temples in many parts of Japan and a complete new city, Tenri, south of the ancient religious centre of Nara. The main sanctuary at Tenri is built around 'the centre of the world', a sacred pillar, and believers both come on pilgrimage and await the dawn of a new age when heavenly dew will descend upon the faithful.

Tenri-kyo, like most other revival movements, had a charismatic founder. Miki had a very troubled early life and after much tribulation she fell into states of trance. She declared that she was possessed by a deity, 'the original true God who has descended from heaven to save all mankind', who required Miki's body as a shrine for its use. Under further fits of possession she gave away all her family goods, but having arrived at complete destitution she manifested miraculous healing powers and believers began to flock to her. Being joined by an efficient organizer, the cult developed and Miki began to compose scriptures, apparently in automatic writing. Tenri-kyo has been notable for its communal spirit, congregational services, and free labour from its members to erect temples and other buildings.

Dr Carmen Blacker of Cambridge, who has made some of the closest studies of Japanese popular and traditional religion, maintains that the so-called 'new religions' are in fact mostly reproductions in modern terms of ancient Japanese religious movements. From time immemorial in Japan, as in many other countries of east and west, there have been cults connected with leaders, shamans or ecstatics. When a new Japanese constitution came into effect in the nineteenth century attempts were made to regulate the religions, separate Shinto and Buddhism which had been mixed for centuries, readmit Christianity, and also separate 'shrine Shinto' from 'sect Shinto'. But it was an artificial distinction, and in times of stress there have always been outbursts of new religious fervour, under various names.

23

This was seen in the depression of the 1930s and after the Second World War.

Most of the popular religions were inspired by a founder, often an ecstatic, who brought a new divine revelation. His or her personal history was one of suffering and perseverance, so giving a model to the followers. Temples or shrines were established, largely under lay organization, and in the community emphasis was placed upon service and self-sacrifice.

Carmen Blacker described some of the traditional pilgrimages and endurance tests that she underwent with bands of faithful. One pilgrimage ended with a ceremony of fire-walking, which is traditional and still practised, in which she herself took part. The embers of a great bonfire were raked out into a red path twenty feet long. Then first the special ascetics strode across the ashes reciting texts, after which it was believed they had made it safe for others. Such a crowd pressed to follow the ascetics that Dr Blacker decided that it would be foolish not to go with them. 'The path was still alarmingly red and smoking by the time my turn came, but . . . the embers underfoot felt no more than pleasantly warm to the soles.' She dismisses explanations that are sometimes offered, such as that Japanese feet are tougher than western ones, or that a quiet and collected mind is needed to walk across unburnt. 'My feet are rather sensitive and my mind at that time was in turmoil, yet a mild warmth was all that I felt.'[2]

Counselling
The popular religions of Japan are group activities, and this is natural in a country where stress is placed upon the family or group rather than on the individual. Further, they are 'lay' religions, in the sense that they run parallel to the more formal and historical Buddhist and Shinto worship. They have inspired

[2] *The Catalpa Bow*, 1975, p. 250f.

leaders, but these are not usually priests or monks. Yet teachings are based upon, or are in general agreement with, traditional Japanese religion, though usually simplified. This is attractive, in that doctrine is made popular and understandable to ordinary people.

The Great Sacred Hall of Rissho Koseikai has a central area which is high-domed and spacious, with a brilliant altar crowned with a great statue of the Buddha. Here communal worship is held, beginning every day and continuing at various times, not only in the hall but wherever believers may be as they turn towards the altar and chant sacred formulas.

Around the Hall are balconies which are lower and more intimate, with plants and flowers. People go by stairs or lifts to the balconies, where floors are carpeted so that shoes are removed as they are in all Japanese homes and sacred buildings. People sit or squat, and children play around, while others come and go as they need. All day long, and every day, there is activity so that the temple provides a religion for all moments and a spacious home for those who live in narrow streets and tiny rooms in the noise and crush of Tokyo.

'Spiritual Counselling' (hoza) is a characteristic activity of Rissho Koseikai. It is paralleled in other Japanese religions, but it is useful to describe it in this particular instance because it has been sympathetically and critically depicted by a Lutheran missionary scholar, Dr Kenneth Dale.

The counsellors are lay teachers, appointed by the community for their ability to teach and lead, and by their words and actions they assume authoritarian postures over their members. The groups they lead are of an average of twelve members or more, chosen from similar neighbourhoods.

'My friend here has acute appendicitis and must have an operation this afternoon, do you think things will turn out all right?' So a member asks in a typical session and receives the reply from the leader, 'Everything depends on your mental

25

attitude. You must talk with your area leader and then go and pray before the altar.'

Another said, 'My husband does not treat me with consideration, and I also have trouble with the lady who lives below us. Why are people so hard to get on with? Why can't I have a good husband and neighbours like other people?' The leader answers, 'Change your mind and repent of this critical attitude towards others, and see the truth of the Law.'

Out of many cases recorded by Dr Dale the main problems discussed in counselling sessions concerned family relations, health, various misfortunes, and work for the religious community. The problems were personal and only rarely raised abstract issues such as the nature of evil or sin. The answers were relatively simple and traditional according to Japanese world views. Questioners were referred to the basic Buddhist doctrine of Karma, 'deeds' and their result, which leads on to reincarnation with rewards or punishments for actions. But the basic Four Noble Truths of Buddhism, which recognize and seek to cure suffering, were put forward.

'A boy had polio and friends wondered why this was and found that his grandfather had been a terrible person. The karma of a former generation was meted out to a later generation.' Further, both Buddhism and Shinto teach veneration to ancestors, they make us 'realize our dependence on those who have gone before and on all other persons and things in the universe'.[3]

The spiritual leader, Mrs Naganuma, who had ecstatic experiences and was a naturally charismatic leader, died in 1957 and there has been greater emphasis since then on institutional efficiency and instruction in doctrine with President Niwano taking the lead. The counselling sessions make a great appeal, with emphasis upon personal religious experience in accepting

[3] *Circle of Harmony*, 1975, pp. 85, 87, 123, 127.

the messages of the leaders, and the change of life which requires the acceptance of suffering as an occasion for repentance and better family relations. The fellowship is of great importance, since people can come to the temples from the struggles of life in great cities and find help and a homely atmosphere. Many of the members of this and similar movements are workers who have often come in from the country, and who struggle with commercial or factory life.

In his considered conclusions to his study Dr Dale emphasizes the development of this new religion amid Japanese traditions, and its adaptation to customs such as sitting on the floor and appealing to devout ancestor veneration. The message is traditional, yet fitted to modern needs. The lay leadership brings a simplified Buddhist teaching, though one that can have limitations, and although there is no priesthood there is a strongly authoritarian direction.

The membership of such movements is chiefly lower middle class, and folk belief and irrational elements of religiosity are evident. The splendid buildings and lavish furnishings show that great contributions of money and work have been made by fairly poor people, but in exchange they receive comfort and instruction. There is a second great hall next to the temple which is devoted to lectures and popular education, and more building is planned. The ostentation and gaudy colouring of the buildings are strikingly different from the restraint and half-tones of Japanese tradition, as seen supremely in the ancient Shinto shrines at Isé. But on the other hand Buddhism has often brought from India and China a love of colour and decoration, and the Japanese have often shown an ability to embrace diverse forms of culture in art and religion.

In conclusion Dr Dale questions some of the methods and treatments of the counselling sessions, criticizing their teachings and authoritarian attitudes. But in the main this Buddhist sect is a movement of renewal, reforming an old religious tradition. 'It is bursting with enthusiasm; its leaders are charismatic; its procedures are disciplined; its message is full of hope; its methods are experimental and experiential.' It is an example to other religions which are struggling for the souls of modern men and women.[4]

Missions?

Watching the procession at the Rissho Koseikai festival, an Australian Unitarian minister among the crowd of honoured guests shouted above the chanting: 'Christianity will never do anything till it puts on a show like this.' It may be doubted whether his own form of intellectualized religion could rise to the challenge, though perhaps Roman Catholicism might provide something comparable, in time.

Christianity in Japan is tiny in numbers, estimated in government statistics at about three million, half of them being Roman Catholic, out of a total population of 110 million. The other half of the Christian population consists chiefly of small sects, many of American and fundamentalist origin. But beyond these statistics there are numbers of unattached people who regard themselves as Christians but have not been baptized, and most important are the so-called Hidden Christians, Kakure Kirishitan, the descendants of converts of the sixteenth century who existed in secret during the persecutions from 1638 to 1865.

In the expansion of European trade in the fifteenth and sixteenth centuries Christian missionaries took part, arriving in Japan in 1549. The most famous was the Jesuit Francis Xavier who, although he stayed in Japan only two years and had difficulty with oriental languages, is said to have had his hands heavy with baptizing. For several decades Roman Catholic missions had considerable success and it has been noted that in no other highly civilized Asian country did Christianity make

---

[4] *Circle of Harmony*, p. 168.

such a mark. The foreign missionaries were at first taken by the Japanese to be a new sect of Buddhists, they secured the protection of powerful rulers, but they regarded the gods of other religions as demons and their worshippers destined for hell.

From 1597 persecutions began, with the crucifixion in Nagasaki of twenty Japanese and six Spanish Christians, Jesuits and Franciscans. Christians had been too successful, rulers saw the dangers of rival movements, and by 1638 all Christians were assumed expelled, killed or forced to recant. Unknown to the authorities, and to the rest of the world, Christian converts continued to practise their faith in secret for over two hundred years, especially in the west and in islands among fishing communities. After the opening of Japan to the West in the nineteenth century and the building of a Roman Catholic church at Oura in Nagasaki small groups of Christians made themselves known to the priests in 1865, although there was still official persecution until a decree of toleration was issued in 1873. The Hidden Christians, without priests, had retained the use of the Lord's Prayer, the Apostles' Creed and the Hail Mary in Japanese, and knew some Japanese and Latin prayers. They celebrated major festivals in secret, and used images of the Buddhist Kannon with a child on her arms, and often marked a cross underneath the image. Some of these Hidden Christians were received into the Roman Catholic church but about thirty thousand prefer to remain with their own organization, largely based on family loyalties.

Perhaps the memory of past persecutions has made other Japanese Christians wary of any compromise with native culture and even more with its religions. Churches in Japan look foreign, in concrete Gothic or drill hall chapel styles. There seem to be no churches in Japanese style, though Fr William Johnston, a Jesuit, makes solitary experiments in a chapel with Japanese decorations, an altar the height of Japanese table altars, and an alcove with a text in Japanese, like traditional alcoves in homes.

On a visit to Japan Dr John Robinson, 'Honest to God' Robinson, and his wife had dinner with us with the President of the International Christian University at Mitaka, Tokyo, the professor of history and two Japanese Christian pastors. We foreigners were trying to find out how much music used in the churches was traditional Japanese. There was a hymn book used in this university chapel, with English on one page and Japanese facing it, the congregation singing in both languages. But since Japanese is a more flowery language than English their words went on beyond the English verses. The music too was Western, Victorian and Moody and Sankey. How many Japanese tunes were there, out of the three hundred hymns? They thought, and answered, four. And how many of these were ancient traditional tunes? One! They were persuaded to sing this hymn, and admitted that they felt it here, with hands on stomachs. Precisely, and only when there is this gut feeling has the religion really taken root.

'All foreigners say that', was the reply. 'We know how to run our own religion.' But if all foreigners say it, there might be some truth in it. As for any adaptation to other religions, look at what Buddhism did. It made its great success by compromise and syncretism, identifying its Buddhas with Shinto gods, and forming a mixed or Twofold Shinto. Christianity should not compromise or contaminate its purity. Or should it?

Chapter Four

SHINTO SILENCE AND SWORD

The Grand Shrine

All day long and every day busloads of pilgrims and tourists arrive in the square outside the grounds of the great shrine of Isé, two hundred miles west of Tokyo, the most holy place in Japan. There is a bustle of holiday, with shops and stalls full of trinkets, and restaurants and inns looking for custom. But when visitors cross the first sacred bridge they become quieter, and especially if there is rain or light mist they try to encourage a spirit of unity with nature.

The first step is through a great plain wooden gateway (*torii*), characteristic of all Shinto shrines, whose massive timbers are made from the largest pillars in the old main buildings of the Inner and Outer Shrines. The gateway, the wooden bridge beyond, and all the main shrine buildings at Isé are demolished and rebuilt every twenty years, a custom going back centuries. Beside the principal shrines there are alternative sites for new buildings and the wood for them is taken from giant cypress trees, some of them hundreds of years old, in the forest in which the shrines stand. In former times discarded wood was burnt but now it is sold to other shrines throughout the country and provides income for the most holy places.

We were fortunate in having as guide a Shinto professor to give a detailed and reverential approach to the shrine. After crossing the bridge over a small but sacred stream, and passing through another gateway at the far end, pilgrims cleanse themselves at a place of water purification. Bamboo cups with long handles rest on laths placed on the stone walls of a rectangular pool through which clear water constantly flows. The cup is first held upside down, then filled with water, the left hand is washed, then the right and the face, and finally water is taken in the mouth to clean it. Beyond the pool there is an opening to the river, also used for purification and full of brightly coloured carp and other fish.

To the right of the washing place is a small fenced enclosure containing only a small stone, which is one of the most primitive sacred objects in the shrine complex. Farther up is a pavilion for two sacred white horses, gifts of the imperial household, which are decked in bright robes and led before the main sanctuary three times a month. Then comes a hall of ritual dance recently rebuilt with a metal framework. The major shrines have no metal, not even nails, but this is not a temple though it is covered with wood when finished to conform to the general appearance of the buildings. Beyond this is a Sacred Kitchen, where food is prepared for the chief shrine and fire is produced by the ancient method of rubbing two pieces of cypress wood together. In a clearing in front of this building, protected only by a rope barrier, lie wooden boxes containing offerings and in the evening they are taken by priests to the major shrine. The boxes are tied to long poles, lifted on to the shoulders of white-robed acolytes, and priests dust the boxes with leaves and sprinkle salt round them while they are carried away in procession.

The southern gate of the Inner Shrine is reached up rough stone steps, at the top of which is the public porch with a gabled roof. White sheets hang over its rear wall and in front is a coffer for gifts, worshippers throwing in small coins, usually the five-yen piece which has a hole in the middle and symbolizes union with the deity. Visitors bow their heads in devotion and clap their hands to attract attention. It is simple worship, with nothing of the sale of lucky paper slips with texts which occupies many other Shinto shrines.

The public can only approach to this outer place at Isé, and a low wooden fence beside it bars entry beyond the door to all but priests and special visitors. The innermost buildings can be seen in the distant enclosures. They are all built of wood, with long projecting roof timbers, and thatched like log cabins though the beam ends are cased in decorated brass shields. In the Inner Shrine is kept the sacred Mirror, the greatest Shinto symbol, which is said to have been presented by the supreme goddess Amaterasu, the sun deity, to her grandson Ninigi when he founded the imperial dynasty of Japan. At his enthronement the emperor goes into the Inner Shrine, traditionally to revere its treasures, though it is said that neither he nor the highest priests ever look upon the mirror. It is kept in a box, which is put into a slightly larger box at each rebuilding of the shrine.

Some four miles separate the Inner Shrine of Isé from the Outer Shrine, which is built on much the same pattern. Traditionally pilgrims walked this road, which is lined with stone lanterns, but now it is tarred and a motor road down which cars and coaches run. In October there is a festival of thanksgiving to Amaterasu at which the first grains of rice from sacred rice-fields are offered to her. The *Japan Times*, one of the English language daily newspapers, prints pictures of the emperor in shirt sleeves, cutting the first rice, after which harvest begins all over the country. An imperial envoy is sent to offer tribute to the deity at Isé, and the priests emerge from a Purification Hall bearing a wooden box containing the gifts. They advance to a great wooden gateway where more priests brush the box with leaves and cast salt around it. The procession, preceded by policemen, takes the box slung on poles, followed by imperial envoys in maroon dress, and perhaps followed by the emperor's daughter, who is a priestess, in white and orange robes. Finally numerous priests march in white robes and black headdresses. When the procession reaches the gate of the Outer Shrine it is opened, the priests pass through and the gate is closed to secular eyes. Observers go to the porch, throw coins into a coffer and stand for a moment with bowed heads.

It is said that some ten million pilgrims visit Isé every year, and going to the shrines is made easier by the flourishing modern tourist industry, taking groups of societies of many kinds. But by five in the evening the cars and coaches leave, restaurants and shops close, and only overnight visitors remain. Then it is the turn of the traditional inns which line the streets outside the shrine enclosure. In front of the inns are rocks, dwarf trees, bushes and decorative lanterns. The lintels of the front doors are of carved wood and along them hang the twisted rice rope and paper strips that mark Shinto places. Shoes are changed at the door for slippers and these too are discarded before stepping on the *tatami* matting of the central room. Tea is served, and ritually drunk, while guests admire the alcove and flower decoration, or gaze out of windows at the sacred river in the quiet of evening.

Isé is a busy yet tranquil place, with the air of quiet and restrained beauty that characterizes Shinto. The site was traditionally chosen in this neighbourhood of hills and trees because it is sheltered from storms, though it has suffered from fierce typhoons. Hunting is forbidden throughout its miles of forest land and rare species of animals are said to flourish. The order and artistry of the thatched log shrines give an air of simplicity and peace. The towering ancient trees, slow clear streams, formal log arches and bridges, and carefully tended buildings and enclosures help relaxation and devotion. This is the most purely Shinto territory in Japan, marked by soft colours and retaining primitive forms, and it is claimed that it has been kept free from Buddhist encroachment during the thirteen hundred years of that religion in the country. Yet in the Shinto museum here Buddhist influence may be noted in Chinese symbols, and at the Great Shrine itself half of the traditional annual dances are of Buddhist and sometimes of Chinese or Indian origin.

Sacred Sword

The second of the three most sacred treasures of Japan, with the mirror at Isé and jewels in Tokyo, is a sacred sword at the Atsuta shrine at Nagoya. Nagoya has the dubious distinction of being the largest industrial city in Japan, though after wartime bombings it was rebuilt with wide streets and it is not so disorderly and ugly as some other modern Japanese cities. But Nagoya is busy and noisy and it comes as a relief to enter the spacious grounds of the Atsuta shrines within the city sprawl. Atsuta-no-okami is the name of the chief deity worshipped here, who is said to be none other than the supreme Amaterasu.

Visitors are received by the shrine secretary and first there is a tea ceremony, turning the cup round, drinking the pale green liquid in three and a half sips, and admiring the pattern made by a celebrated potter. At a hall of ceremony mothers bring children to be blessed. Little girls of three, five and seven, in bright kimonos and with flowers in their hair, arrive with their parents. In the hall they present gifts, and priestesses in white and red robes perform slow dances of blessing with fans, to the accompaniment of musicians who sit at the side of the stage beating drums.

The chief Atsuta shrine, like those at Isé, can only be glimpsed in the distance beyond low bamboo fences. The buildings are again like thatched log cabins, with long projecting roof beams and chastely decorated ends. The sacred sword is there, though visitors do not see it. However the shrine treasure hall has many fine swords on display, made by craftsmen over the centuries.

Atsuta is popular for tea ceremonies and there are small huts where these take place as religious rituals, with queues waiting their turn. Weddings are also celebrated, though these are often performed in the home and not in temple or shrine. But at Atsuta there are expensive weddings, with brides in brilliant costumes and elaborate headdresses, while their prospective husbands are in dull grey and black robes or suits.

By some clever move in the past Shinto has cornered the life-giving ceremonies, of childhood and marriage, and left funerals to the Buddhists. The latter probably found that chanting verses from the endless Buddhist scriptures ensured them an income, and teachings about the bliss of Nirvana or the Pure Land of Amida may have been more comforting than vague Shinto notions of a future only palely reflecting life on this earth. The two religions, so often mingled, appeal to varied needs.

Shinto is native to Japan and restricted to it, so that it is often neglected in studies of world religions, yet seen at first hand it has surprising extent and vitality. The whole country is said to be under the care of one or other of the Shinto shrines, of which there are about a hundred thousand, like parish churches in the western world. It is claimed also that no shrine is destroyed, though it may be moved, yet it is difficult to test this claim and it may be that in the vast cities older shrines have been swallowed up.

In addition to the great and extensive shrines, at Isé, Atsuta and Izumo, there are innumerable small shrines, in towns and villages, public places and gardens, all marked with the characteristic *torii* gateway. The altars of Shinto shrines have no images, only hollow boxes into which it is thought the divinity may descend. Imagery, like stone building for temples, came with Buddhism from Korea and China, but despite Buddhist influence Shinto retains some of its original simplicity.

The very name Shinto is foreign, being the Chinese term for 'the Way of the Gods', to distinguish it from 'the Way of the Buddha'. The Japanese use Chinese characters for Shinto, but pronounce them 'Kami-no Michi', their version of 'the Way of the Gods'. Before the Chinese-Buddhist arrival in Japan in the sixth century A.D. there was Shinto, and traditions but no literature, for Buddhist monks brought writing to Japan as Christian monks spread writing over Europe. Buddhism was favoured by some rulers and became dominant in much of medieval Japanese history, a mixed (Ryobu) Shinto-Buddhism prevailing, yet Shinto remained at the root of Japanese culture and has been revived since the last century.

Religion and State

In 1978 the first public performance of *The Mikado* was given in Toyko. Gilbert and Sullivan's comic opera had delighted western audiences for nearly a century, but it had been too irreverent, if not derisive, for the Japanese, though there had been a few private performances for foreigners. Presentation of the even more light-hearted *Black Mikado* was out of the question in this country.

Mikado, 'august door' of the palace, is a title used since the tenth century, though normally Japanese prefer the more ancient and sonorous Tenno, 'heavenly ruler', which links the emperor to his first human ancestor and to the sun deity Amaterasu herself. Shinto was the religion of Japan, and the emperor its high priest, though in the imperialistic and colonizing expansion of Japan some writers thought of Shinto as destined to become a world religion under the one emperor. The divine origin and nature of the emperor was held fervently for centuries, and probably still is cherished by many people, but in a 'Human Declaration' at the end of the war in 1945 an Imperial Rescript publicly renounced 'the false conception that the Emperor is divine'.

Mixed feelings are still evident in many ways, illustrating the tensions between the tradition of divine authority, like the Chinese Mandate of Heaven, and modern democratic notions of sovereignty. In the autumn of 1977 Emperor Hirohito gave his first-ever news conference, in which he referred to the Human Declaration but treated it as subordinate to the Charter Oath and constitution of 1868 which had asserted that 'all classes, high and low, shall unite in vigorously carrying out the administration of affairs of state'. The *Japan Times* headed its report of this conference 'History from the Horse's Mouth', a phrase that might surprise even a democratic monarchist.

I had got to know the emperor's younger brother, Prince Mikasa, some years before when we had both received honorary degrees of Doctor of Letters from the University of Lancaster. He had been a professor of comparative religion in Tokyo Women's Christian College, and later we accompanied him to Nagoya and were given a civic reception and an entertainment by the Shinto university there. At a further conference a Japanese lecturer gave a penetrating study of the development of the imperial tradition and ended by comparing it with western constitutional monarchies. These depend upon the consent of the people governed, and no longer upon any 'divine right of kings', or claim descent from a divine ancestor. He turned to Prince Mikasa and asked pointblank whether he believed that imperial authority depended upon the agreement of the people. Put on the spot, the prince broke his normal reserve and replied judiciously, 'I think so, but I cannot say what the rest of my family think'.

Old and new, religion and politics, are mingled in Japan, perhaps more clearly than in some other countries. The emperor is a constitutional monarch, of a kind. He wears western dress and, it is said, prefers western food to the traditional Japanese. Yet he is the chief official of Shinto and every year performs twenty-seven rituals whose origins and meaning go back to ancient times.

When Shinto was disestablished as a state religion in 1945, the separation of religion and state was instituted. But this was not accepted easily by some of the great national shrines and attempts have continually been made to obtain state funds for places of national importance. Christian, Buddhist and secular writers have vigorously opposed such moves, regarding them as efforts to obtain a favoured position for Shinto, and opposition has centred on efforts made by the officers of the Yasukuni shrine in Toyko.

The Yasukuni Jinja ('nation-protecting' *jinja*, 'shrine', the term used to distinguish Shinto from Buddhist temples) was established in 1869 'to venerate the loyal spirits' of those who died in the struggle to establish the new regime in 1868 in place of the feudalism which had isolated Japan for centuries from the rest of the world. But the shrine has extended its purpose to include, according to the official notice, 'all who have since made the supreme sacrifice for their country', irrespective of the cause or occasion. The notice further declares that 'the rites observed in sanctuary are to console their spirits. Those who worship here daily and the thousands who worship at the Grand Festival in spring and autumn are mainly for the bereaved families throughout the nation who cherish their memory.'

The problem of distinguishing religious worship from veneration of ancestors and respect for the recently departed, is revealed acutely here. Christian missions have often struggled with this question, and the Jesuits in China maintained for centuries that ancestor reverence was not religious worship and could be continued by their converts. They had considerable success, though due to rivalry from other Roman Catholic orders this practice of toleration came to be forbidden, to the loss of many followers. In Japan the small Christian churches officially oppose the recognition of or participation in ceremonies at Shinto shrines ancestral or other. They have memories of sufferings before and during the Second World War when some Christians resisted orders to bow to pictures of the emperor and reverence the nation at the nearest Shinto shrine.

The Yasukuni shrine appears a rather heavy-handed example of civic architecture, traditional and modern. Its massive *torii* gateway is sixteen metres high and said to be the largest in Japan, yet it is in granite and not in the unpolished wood of the ancient shrines. Its pavilions are in Chinese Buddhist style, without its grace or colour. No doubt the officials would welcome Christians and others at the ancestral veneration, and some may go there for this purpose, but there seems no reason why it should be maintained by the state since it has many visitors and is self-supporting.

Chrysanthemum and Sword

The foreigner in Japan, if he can stay beyond a few days or weeks, soon becomes aware of paradoxes and contradictions. There is great politeness and much bowing, which disappear when fighting for a place on an underground railway train. There is scrupulous cleanliness in the home, where shoes are always doffed, but there is often dirt in public places. There is kindness and hospitality in public entertainment, but it is rare that one is received into a home. There is modernism and irreligion, and Japan has been called the most secularized nation in Asia. Yet we have seen the appeal both of the Isé shrines and of the new religious movements, and sixty or seventy million are said to go to temples and tombs at the New Year holidays.

The Japanese are different, it is often said, and different seems to imply better. Japan was isolated from the rest of Asia for centuries and regarded itself as superior, though it owed much of its culture to China, and in recent imperialistic adventures tried to rule much of eastern Asia. One Japanese professor has even claimed that the Japanese brain is different or used differently from that of the rest of mankind, for it needs to use both reason and emotion of the two sides of the brain for its very difficult language. Even the Christian churches, usually anxious to be completely different from Shinto and Buddhism, reject traditional architecture and music but resent suggestions for a broader culture in a kind of defensive nationalism.

Ruth Benedict, a famous American anthropologist,

illustrated some of the paradoxes in her book *The Chrysanthemum and the Sword*. Written at the end of the Second World War, the book tried to explain the harshness and robot-like discipline of the army, under which many foreign prisoners had suffered, contrasted with a passion for western ways. There has been a cult of aestheticism which honoured artists and cultivated chrysanthemums, cherry blossoms and tea ceremonies, and on the other hand there has been the rule of the Samurai warriors and the cult of the sword.

Paradoxes continue in religious affairs. Official statistics state that Shinto has 84 million adherents and Buddhism 83 million, out of a total population for Japan of 110 million. This is accounted for by many people resorting to both religions for different occasions in life. Revivalism in Buddhist and Shinto sects adds to the complex religious scene.

From the eighteenth century there was a Shinto revival, reacting against the medieval dominance of Buddhism in Japanese political and intellectual life, and rejecting the Twofold Shinto wherein Buddhists ruled both temples and shrines. But along with attempts at providing intellectual apologetics for Shinto, there went a nationalism which led too easily to the identification of religion and state, and the justification of warfare and imperialistic expansion. Shinto, which had been basically a nature and ancestral religion, could thus be made into a political tool. The problem of Shinto nowadays is to find new grounds for its self-expression, which can appeal to modern educated men and women.

In the south-western island of Kyushu there is a famous shrine, the Dazaifu Tenman-gu, whose chief priest is a Harvard-educated man who has seen developments for Shinto in the modern world and in the future. Dazaifu is an ancient centre, founded in the seventh century, and the principal shrine commemorates a distinguished Confucian scholar of two centuries later. After his death and memorial ceremonies, he gradually became deified and is claimed as 'Honourable Divine God' and patron of calligraphic studies.

Like most old Shinto shrines this one is set among trees, gardens, streams and bridges. There are graceful old buildings, and modern halls. But in addition to the shrines and ceremonies, the literature claims attention. For here this Shinto priest begins to face some of the problems of his religion in modern times. 'The Shinto world', he writes, 'was greatly changed after the war'. He reviews some of the struggles of a suddenly disestablished religion, the question of the Yasukuni shrine, the wider interest taken nowadays in understanding Shinto. He concludes with a statement of the aims of Shinto teachers in the future: Shinto needs to express the feelings of the community, it requires both an ancestral and a personal faith, it has cultural functions in preserving past customs and adapting to new phenomena, and it must not only express native ideas but 'develop a universal humanistic character—not a nationalistic one'.[1]

[1] *Dazaifu Tenman-gu*, p. 156f.

Chapter Five

HARE KRISHNA

His Divine Grace
In 1973 I received a letter from ISKCON, the International
Society for Krishna Consciousness, saying that its founder,
Acharya: His Divine Grace A. C. Bhaktivedanta Swami
Prabhupada, 'one of the world's leading Vedic philosophers'
was staying in London for several months. Every evening he
was receiving one or two guests to have dinner and enjoy an
informal exchange of ideas, and 'among his recent guests are Sir
Alister Hardy, Arnold Toynbee, Allen Ginsberg, and Dr
Ramsey, Archbishop of Canterbury.' He would be honoured
by a visit and would arrange transport.

The headquarters of this society was at Bhaktivedanta
Manor, formerly Piggot's Manor, a mock-Tudor building of
some fifty rooms, set in seventeen acres at Letchmore Heath in
Hertfordshire. It was given to the society by former Beatle
George Harrison, once a follower of the rival Guru, Maharishi
Mahesh Yogi of Transcendental Meditation. Here had been
founded 'a practising self-sufficient community' whose object
was to display to the world 'the attraction of the Vedic lifestyle',
which could be summarised as 'simple living and high thinking
based on the realisation that the goal of life is to redevelop a
personal relationship with God.'

I went and met the leader, greeting him as Swami, an Indian
title for a spiritual leader or pundit, and less difficult
theologically than Divine Grace. Colin Cross, in an article in
The Observer, had described his own meeting with the Swami
and called it 'an unnerving experience'. Perhaps he was easily
impressed, though apparently he only gave the Swami a polite
nod and squatted cross-legged on the floor. But chairs were

available and no attempt was made to bemuse or intimidate the visitor. The Swami was revered, of course, by his disciples, who prostrated themselves on entering the audience room and then sat quickly round the wall.

Swami Bhaktivedanta was claimed in the literature of his community as 'the leading exponent of the science of Krishna consciousness in the West and the world's most distinguished teacher of Vedic religion and thought.' But there are many Indian scholars who teach a non-dualistic or pantheistic interpretation of the philosophy of the Upanishads, the original Vedanta and later interpretations. Bhakti-vedanta indicates a mingling of non-dualistic philosphy with the religious fervour of 'bhakti', devotion or love to God.

At the Manor the Swami lolled back on cushions and discussion began, or rather he discoursed, often with eyes shut, hardly stopping for two hours. Occasionally it was possible to get a question in: What had Toynbee and the Archbishop said? Oh, they had not been yet. But perhaps they had been asked, and no doubt some other notables had paid visits, like Colin Cross and Malcolm Muggeridge. What did the Swami think of the teachings of the rival Mahesh Yogi of Transcendental Meditation? With true religious dogmatism he retorted that they were wrong interpretations. Maharishi Mahesh (self-styled Great-seer, Great-lord) was a non-dualist or pantheist, whereas the Swami taught ardent devotion to the personal God Krishna.

The Swami quoted the famous Indian classic, the Bhagavad Gita, the Song of the Lord (Krishna) frequently, but when asked which of the fifty or so English translations he preferred, only his was acceptable. Professor R. C. Zaehner's scholarly translation and long commentary was declared to be inadequate, for he was a Catholic and did not believe in Krishna and so could not expound his teachings. Dr Radhakrishnan, late President of India, had made a translation and commentary of the Gita, but this was too pantheistic, as was Mahesh Yogi's.

The Swami's own English translation, with Sanskrit text, romanized transliteration, English translation, and commentary, is *Bhagavad-gītā as it is*. It is claimed as 'the most complete and authoritative transmission of this timeless scripture in print and the only one that does not obscure the true spirit of Krishna's teachings.'

A great deal of the finances and activities of this movement seems to come from publications. The Swami rose early each morning to begin translation and commentary. He was now engaged on a version of another great and popular Krishna classic, the Bhagavata Purana, which has never been fully translated into English. It seems that he translated and commented verbally, his words being recorded and then typed out. The work is very long and some fifty volumes were planned, of which about a dozen have appeared so far. But the circulation seems to be extensive, with printings of about thirty thousand for each volume, at ten dollars or more a volume. That is big money, as every publisher knows, if there is guaranteed subscription.

This version of the Gita is 'illustrated with forty-four magnificent full-color paintings—original works painted especially for this volume.' These seem gaudy and amateurish, like popular bazaar prints in India, and it was suggested that it would be an improvement to use some of the graceful illustrations to the Krishna story from classical Indian artists of Rajasthan or the Punjab hills, which are available in great museums and galleries. But it was replied that the pictures in the book are by an American devotee and they come better from a believer.

Swami and Devotees
It is said that Swami Bhaktivedanta was a chemist in India for many years, though also a student and teacher of religion. He was sixty-nine when he arrived in New York with little money,

but from the foundation of his community in 1966 it has spread widely. The Swami came to control a large organization and was regarded with great veneration by many young people. He died in 1977.

'Hare Krishna, Hare Krishna, Lord Krishna, Hail Krishna', these cries with musical accompaniments have been heard in many cities of the western world in recent years. Young men and women in saffron robes, the men with heads shaven except for the topknot, carry prayer beads and musical instruments. They chant, distribute leaflets, sell books, collect money, and eagerly talk about Lord Krishna.

Who are these young men and women? At Letchworth there was a community of about sixty men, women and children; some married couples and others celibate. There was strict discipline and, like many religious movements in their beginnings, there was Puritanism alongside ecstatic religious fervour. Chastity was decreed, with vegetarianism and a ban on smoking, alcohol, coffee, tea and other stimulants. The disciples seemed to be mostly young Americans, ardent in veneration of their Guru, defending his lightest word, and extreme in reverence for everything Indian. One was a lapsed Irish Catholic, but that seemed unusual.

Why had these young people accepted this exotic and ecstatic form of religion, and why could not Christianity appeal to them? The two questions are related, but the first may be particularly involved with modern social conditions. The revolt of western, especially American, youth against the dull and 'square' customs of their parents is well known. The 'American dream' resulted for many in material success, luxury undreamed of by the pioneers, leading to the virtual worship of money and power. Many young people rebelled against this, and instead of being content to go into business and make more money, they sought for colour and meaning to life. Much of the work of their elders seemed to be like that of the dung beetles in the *Insect*

Play, making one pile of dung and then going off to make another pile.

The revolt was against materialism, and formal religion and politics, but not against more exciting forms of religion. In previous decades there had come knowledge of Asian religious teachings, especially the pantheistic philosophy of Hinduism or the near-atheistic philosophy of Buddhism. This can be illustrated from an anthology called *Vedanta for Modern Man*, with contributions from Aldous Huxley, Isherwood and Heard, which expounded pantheistic identity with the universe, or pointed to the 'void' of Buddhist philosophy.

Now Hare Krishna and similar movements reacted against this philosophical vacuity and looked for the exciting, exotic and beautiful. More recent movements, such as that of Bhagvan Rajneesh, have become even more voluptuous. Personal and emotional religion came back into its own, with the glamour of medieval Catholicism or the revivalism of early Methodism.

Why did not Christianity appeal to these young rebels? One answer is in the above; it was seen, by many at least, as traditional, dull and formal. But if an exciting version was presented, as in *Godspell* or *Jesus Christ Superstar*, it had great popularity. There are vital new Christian movements, Charismatics for example who believe in divine inspiration and often speak with tongues, which sweep across America and Europe, among Protestants and Catholics. Dry rational movements, like Unitarianism, have declined, while Pentecostalism has flourished.

Oriental teachers have not been slow to cash in on this market, which has been opened up by the easy communications of the modern world, and the knowledge of many religions that has come from studies in comparative religion. On a popular level, the idea has spread that the East is mysterious and spiritual, while the West is materialistic. Many young people have gone to Asia, and some have become disillusioned by the poverty and dirt. In the reverse direction there has almost been an export trade from India in sending Gurus to the West, and some of the most successful have become business managers of large spiritual organizations. Christian missions have long been preaching in Asia, and so these Indian Gurus are returning the compliment by missionizing the West.

On the other hand, in many countries of Asia and Africa Christianity is exotic and attractive. It is said that the New Testament is quoted more often in newspapers in India and Japan than in the Christian West. Perhaps that is not difficult, and the Bible appeals to eastern people in its freshness, its Asian character, and its high moral and spiritual teachings. The West may be Gospel-hardened, having received and then often stifled the peaceful and mystical verses of the New Testament. Meanwhile Hare Krishna and other cults attract those hungry sheep that are not fed by the dry husks distributed by church managers.

Indian Religion

I had been to India a number of times before I went to Japan, and was impressed by the many temples and monuments, philosphies and religions. Krishna is very different from the Buddha, and while the appeal of Buddhism has been felt in the West for over a hundred years, the call of Krishna and Hinduism there is a relatively modern development. Yet the Buddha was an Indian and basic Buddhist ideas, such as Karma and reincarnation, are Hindu. And Hinduism is all-embracing, so that while Krishna is said to be an Avatar or 'down-coming' of the great god Vishnu, in course of time the Buddha was also recognized as an Avatar. In this way Buddhists were won back to Hinduism, and Buddhism virtually disappeared from the land of its birth.

The visitor to India may feel like Paul in Athens, saying, 'I perceive that in every way you are very religious'. For there are countless temples with sculptures, images and pictures of all manner of gods. There was no historical founder of Hinduism, like the Buddha or Muhammad for other religions. There have been reformers, like the philosopher Shankara or the founder of Sikhism, Guru Nanak, but much of ancient and unreformed Hinduism has persisted until modern times.

Hinduism is sometimes claimed as the world's oldest religion, though Hebrew religion may have as good a claim and Zoroaster may have been contemporary with the Hindu Vedic scriptures. But age does not guarantee the highest developments and both reformation and new ideas may be needed. In the chief temples of the fierce goddess Kali in Calcutta animal sacrifice still takes place and visitors may be asked to pay for a goat. President Radhakrishnan said that it was a pity Shankara did not include the Kali temples among his reforms and most Indians would agree, since many of them are vegetarians and object to taking any form of life. The great Indian emperor Ashoka in the third century B.C. forbade killing any animals, for food or sacrifice.

Krishna is one of the most popular of the many gods of India, the lofty deity of the classic Bhagavad Gita and the only God to many of his followers. For among the many divinities many people worship only one God, or regard the others as his manifestations, or see them as aspects of the neutral divine being Brahman. The name Krishna means 'black', and he may represent the survival and reform of an ancient religion of the darker peoples of southern India which became popular all over the sub-continent. In devotional cults Krishna is the divine lover, and the strongly erotic element in some of his stories surprised and offended some foreign observers and certain Indian reformers. Yet the love and passion expressed in the worship of Krishna have attracted millions of Indians down the ages, as symbolical of the love of God and the human soul.

The romantic stories of Krishna are told in Puranas, 'ancient

49

tales', which are more popular than the abstract Gita. These narratives delight in the miraculous and mischievous childhood of Krishna, and they inspire women in particular in their devotions to images of baby Krishna. As he grew up, say the Puranas, he had adventures with cowherds, drove out the calves, flirted with milkmaids, hid their clothes while they bathed, danced with his paramours, eloped with his favourite Radha, deserted her and hid away, and then returned in triumph to rule with a vast family for many ages. Finally he was wounded by Old Age, abandoned his mortal body, and re-entered the celestial sphere as the god Vishnu of whom he was the Avatar. All this is illustrated in countless stories, and pictures of Krishna's adventures are found in temples, homes and books. They inspire and direct worship, dance, song and pilgrimage.

A Roman Catholic priest, Klaus Klostermaier, lived for two years in Vrindaban, one of the most popular places of Krishna pilgrimage in northern India and the traditional site of the love-play of Krishna with the milkmaids. He has described sharing in processions and devotions, and the great crowds that come every year as to Krishna's paradise, the place where the highest degree of love for Krishna can be attained. 'The clear and loud voices of the little children and the harsher, deeper ones of the men, the strong voices of the village women and the reserved, soft voices of the genteel ladies—all of them sang the praises of Krishna and Radha and all of them went this way in search of greater love for him, perhaps even to behold him in reality.'[1]

Another Roman Catholic priest has written of the popular god Shiva, who has also caused offence to westerners because of his fierce and erotic actions in mythology and his representation in phallic symbolism all over India still. Shiva is regarded by his followers, distinct from those of Vishnu and Krishna, as both creator and destroyer, Lord of the Dance, Lord of Yogis, Master

[1] *Hindu and Christian in Vrindaban*, 1969, p. 15.

of Animals, Vanquisher of Death. He does not descend into the world of Avatars, but he is believed to appear in grace to his faithful followers. Writing of the teachers and worshippers of Shiva this priest stresses their 'strict monotheism', with its 'single-minded and undivided love to the unique Supreme Being'.[2]

To understand Hinduism, both in India and as exported to the West by travelling Gurus, knowledge and sympathy are needed. On the other hand it would be false kindness to close one's eyes to the extreme fantasies and wild actions, the fierce passions and the intolerance, that sometimes mar such emotional religions. From an ethical point of view they may seem to be immoral, and from a philosophical viewpoint superstitious, 'the opiate of the people', yet at best they may express universal longings. Kipling again saw a common humanity here,

> 'My brother kneels (so saith Kabir)
>   To stone and brass in heathen-wise,
> But in my brother's voice I hear
>   My own unanswered agonies.
> His God is as his Fates assign—
> His prayer is all the world's—and mine.'

The Wisdom of the Forest
Early in the first millenium B.C., perhaps before the first Greek philosophers, men and women in India meditated and speculated about the nature of the world and the human soul. Military invasions and tribal squabbles had settled down and by great rivers like the Indus and the Ganges walled citites were built, crafts and arts developed, and there was leisure from the struggle for existence to consider what it meant. Some ascetics went into the depths of the jungle to overcome nature and their

[2] M. Dhavamony, *Love of God according to Śaiva Siddhānta*, 1971, p. 337.

own passions, but many others settled in open country, ideally under a tree, near a river, attended by a wife or students and, as the Buddhists put it, 'with a village nearby for support'.

At times great rulers, like a famous king Janaka, held philosophical tournaments to which many sages were invited. One of the most celebrated, with the difficult name of Yajnya-valkya, was a sort of Indian Socrates or Confucius. He also had a sense of humour, and when Janaka offered a thousand cows with gold pieces on their horns to the best philosopher, Yajnya-valkya told his own pupil to drive them to his home at once. 'Are you the best scholar?' asked Janaka's priest. 'Probably', he replied, 'but I just want to have those cows'.

The other assembled philosophers questioned Yajnya-valkya in a series of debates which are recorded in the Upanishads, 'sitting-down-near', sessions of thought, perhaps dating from the eighth to the fifth centuries B.C. They plunge straightaway into the agelong question, 'when a man dies what is there that remains?' Yajnya-valkya first of all said it was his works, *karma*, for 'one becomes good by good action, and evil by evil action.' Later a man was compared with a tree, but whereas a tree may shoot up again man does not. Later still the soul after death is compared to the spirit that wanders in dreams, creating its own world of roads and bridges, or it is like a piece of gold which can be changed into a more beautiful ornament, or it is like a caterpillar which comes to the end of a blade of grass and draws itself up to enter another blade as the soul passes to another life.

Another sage, Uddalaka, made many sacrifices to gain merit, but he was criticized by his son, Nachiketas, for sacrificing barren cattle. The boy offered himself, 'Papa, why not offer me?' and finally in exasperation his father retorted, 'Go to Hades, I will offer you to Death.' Apparently the boy was sacrificed, as Isaac almost was by Abraham. He went to the world beyond to meet the king of death, Yama, who happened to be away for three days. On his return Death offered the young man three boons to compensate for not having received the courtesies due to visitors. The first two boons were formal and easily granted but the third was the perennial question, asking Death, 'what happens after death? some say a man exists, some say he does not, I want to settle the matter.' Death tried to evade the question by offering many other presents, but Nachiketas persisted and at length Death came out with a renowned answer, which was quoted later almost verbatim in the Bhagavad Gita. This is the assertion, an intuition, of the eternity or indestructibility of the soul, it always exists, without beginning or end.

> 'The soul never dies and is never born,
> came not into being, and never comes to be,
> primeval, not slain when the body dies,
> unborn, eternal, everlasting.'[3]

Other dialogues consider the immediate fate of the soul at death. If it survives, how is it that heaven is not full up? the kind of question an intelligent child might put in school. Uddalaka again is asked this and confesses his ignorance. He is instructed by a ruler, who asserts that this knowledge had been kept by the princely classes and that the priestly Brahmins had not known it, a hint perhaps of a different religious or racial tradition. The answer to this question is that of rebirth, transmigration or reincarnation. Those who die and are cremated rise up to the sky, and receive the rewards of their deeds, but then they return in the wind and the rain, enter into herbs and plants, are eaten as food and reborn into another womb. But the kind of birth is determined by their previous karma. Those of previous good conduct will enter the wombs of women of priestly, princely or merchant classes, the three top castes. Those of bad conduct will enter foul wombs, of a bitch, a sow, or an outcaste woman.

[3] see *The Wisdom of the Forest*, 1975, p. 73.

The doctrine of reincarnation enunciated here was probably very old in India, characteristic of Hinduism but being taught by other Indian religions and spreading with Buddhism right across Asia. It is distinctive of 'eastern' religions but has been unknown to or rejected by western religions, Christianity, Judaism and Islam. Yet Plato in a story at the end of his Republic has a similar tale of a man who goes to the afterworld and sees souls being rewarded or punished according to their deeds and then reborn on earth. 'It was a truly wondrous sight, to watch how each soul selected its life'. And to the objection that we do not remember our past lives, though some claim they do, Plato said that when the souls had chosen their lives they had to travel through the Plain of Forgetfulness and drink of the River of Indifference so that they forget everything. The Upanishads, like Plato, do not claim memory as evidence of previous lives. For them the proof is in the very nature of the soul, which is never born and never dies, pre-existence as well as post-existence, in fact constant existence.

There are many other dialogues and questions in the Upanishads. Yajnya-valkya tackled the question of the many gods, 3,306 according to tradition, by reducing them all to thirty-three, six, three, two, one and a half, and one. What is that one God? It is the Breath of Life, Being, they call it That.

Uddalaka asserted the primacy of conscious Being. Some people say that in the beginning the universe was simply Non-being, and Being arose out of it. But that could not be so. How could Being come out of Non-being? No, it was alone in the beginning, one only, without a second. In a series of nine dialogues Uddalaka taught that the subtle essence of the universe is the Soul or Self, and you are that self. In tiny seeds nothing can be seen but they contain an essence from which trees grow. When salt is put in water it cannot be seen, but its essence is there. Rivers flow into the sea and cannot be distinguished yet their essence is there. Nine times the sage concluded his examples with the assertion, 'That subtle essence is the Soul of the whole universe. That is Reality, That is the Soul. *You* are That.'

This famous phrase 'That thou art' (*tat twam asi*), 'you are that very Soul', 'You're It', or 'you the individual soul are the soul of the universe', has given rise to endless discussion. The later Vedantic philosophers, commenting on the Vedanta, the Veda's End or Upanishads, divided roughly into three schools. Shankara taught entire non-dualism, not-twoness, you are the divine, the ultimate Brahman beyond the gods. Ramanuja taught a 'qualified non-dualism', recognizing a difference between 'you' and 'That', since religion requires a difference between the soul and God, even when it is part of the Body of God. Madhva taught frank dualism, and interpreted the text to mean 'you are not That'.

One of the later classical Upanishads puts the problem in a more religious context: 'What is the cause of everything? Is it Time that is the cause? or Nature? or Fate? or Accident? or the Elements? or a male or female being? or a combination of all these? No, it cannot be so, because of the existence of the Soul. The sage proceeds to speak of a cosmic being, a gracious Creator. 'Some sages say that Nature was the first Cause, and others that it was Time. Both are deluded, for it is the greatness of God in the world that caused everything to exist and move.' He is the One that encompasses the universe, intelligent, omniscient, commanding all actions, ruling over transmigration, the inner soul of all beings.[4]

This provides the transition from philosophical speculation to religious assertion, notably in the Bhagavad Gita. For most Hindus it is not the priestly texts of the Vedas, or even the philosophical discourses of the Upanishads and later that are known and understood, but the heroic and divine stories of the

[4] *The Wisdom of the Forest*, p. 90f.

epic poems and Puranas. Many educated Hindus know little of the ancient texts, and the Sanskrit language in which they were preserved had almost been forgotten until modern times.

Over tea in his home in Delhi President Radhakrishnan talked with me about the problems of studying different religions and teaching them. As in his books, he quoted widely from writings of many of the world's religions, east and west. He also emphasized the value of the Sanskrit language in the study of Hindu philosophy and theology, and his own translations from Sanskrit of the Upanishads and the Bhagavad Gita have been widely used.

Especially in the last two centuries, the Bhagavad Gita, a small section of the great epic poem Mahabharata, has been cherished by educated Indians and by other people in many countries. Mahatma Gandhi said, 'I find a solace in the Bhagavad Gita and Upanishads that I miss even in the Sermon on the Mount.' Yet the Gita is not without its difficulties and some of these will be considered next.

Chapter Six

THE GITA, STOPES AND ZAEHNER

Gita as Word of God

Christians, Jews and Muslims are used to thinking of their scriptures as the Word of God, distinctive and perhaps unique. But Indian and farther eastern religions have been spoken of, from the outside, as pantheistic if not atheistic, and their scriptures as human compositions, man raising himself by his own efforts. Yet in Hinduism, for example, the Vedas are regarded as revealed or 'heard' (*shruti*) by the ancient seers from the gods, and later texts are 'remembered' (*smriti*) though providing guidance and inspiration.

The hymns of the Vedas, however, are psalms which priests chanted in praise of the deities, imploring them to receive sacrifices, and though it may be presumed that the gods were thought to answer their words are not recorded. The addresses are godward, not words given to men. The speculations of the Upanishads are tentative and intuitive, tending towards a monistic pantheism but hardly providing divine revelation. The classic declaration 'thou art That' excludes divine–human dialogue, at least in the non–dualistic interpretation.

In the Bhagavad Gita, however, God speaks to man in what has been called the first time in Hinduism. It has also been called the last, but account must be taken of many scriptures and prayers which imply answers. In the long epic poem of the Mahabharata, a small section in the sixth book contains this important work called the 'Song' (Gita) of the 'Lord' (Bhagavat) Krishna. It is all in verse, but each section is prefaced 'the Blessed Lord said', and in response to the problems of his devotee Krishna sings his teachings in a sort of plain chant.

God speaks to man in the Gita and he is God with a capital G.

For although other gods are mentioned they are all parts of his pervading powers or supernal manifestations, he is in them all and far beyond. He is hailed as Primal God, First Creator, Lord of gods, greater than Brahman, the supreme resting-place of the universe. He is Krishna, and given many titles, though only in the great central vision of chapter eleven is he fully identified with Vishnu. He is the lofty, gracious yet impassive Krishna, with none of the erotic elements of later stories.

This God appears in visible form in the world (chapter 4, 6–9):

> 'Whenever there is a languishing of right (*dharma*)
> and a growth of unrighteousness (*adharma*),
> then I send forth myself by my own power.'

This is the doctrine of the Avatar, the 'descent' or manifestation of the deity (see later), although the word Avatar is not used. The God comes into the world, with the purpose of putting down evil and restoring good.

Other verses (3, 22–24) declare that God does not need to gain anything and has nothing yet to attain, but he continues in action for if he did not the world would perish, and so his example should be followed. This is rather like the argument whether God really rested on the seventh day, for if he had done the universe would have collapsed, and Jesus justified healing on the Sabbath by saying, 'my Father works even till now, and so do I'.

Chapter eleven of the Gita is called the Vision of the Universal Form, and it is probably the most lengthy, detailed and terrifying vision of God in all religious literature. It was from here that an atomic scientist quoted when the first nuclear bomb was exploded in the Nevada desert with 'the splendour of a thousand suns' (11, 12). Yet it is remarkable that when the disciple, the warrior Arjuna, is frightened at the sight of the colossal and fearful Krishna-Vishnu, he has a feeling of unworthiness. He has been too familiar with the visible Krishna, his charioteer, in play, rest, eating and sitting, privately and publicly. He begs forgiveness and prostrates himself, the vision has been too much and he pleads for the return of the human Krishna, and in response the God comforts his friend and turns again into his gracious form. This leads on to the 'love' (*bhakti*) which man must show to God, and which then God manifests to him, telling him at the end that he is 'dear beyond measure' and 'loved exceedingly' (18, 64).

Some of the other teachings of the Gita, among its many themes and especially its ethical views, are now to be considered.

Marie Stopes's Copy

For nearly twenty years I taught the Bhagavad Gita in English as part of a university course and made a translation of it. I began collecting other versions and one day picked up an edition of *The Geeta, The Gospel of the Lord Shri Krishna* by Shri Purohit Swami, published in 1935. On the fly leaf was a book plate Ex Libris M. C. C. Stopes and a bold pencil signature of Marie C. Stopes.

Marie Stopes had been notorious as a pioneer of birth control clinics, from 1921 to her death in 1958. Her book *Married Love*, which advocated birth control, caused a storm of controversy though it was translated into thirteen languages, including Hindi, yet it was banned in some states of the United States. It was interesting to speculate on why the champion of *Married Love* and passionate desire should have read such an ascetic work as the Gita, but she provided a useful example of a religiously-minded European lay person attracted to but critical of a great Indian classic and she revealed some of the problems of studying this scripture.

Marie Stopes had the habit of marking books with strong

pencil lines and comments, helpful for the reader since they revealed her reactions. She was a devoutly religious woman, despite or because of her views, and the early pages of her *Geeta* were marked with reverent underlining as the tedious lists of warriors were noted. Some verses were encircled in pencil for greater merit, such as 'What were a kingdom or happiness or life to me?', and 'when irreligion spreads, the women of the house begin to stray', and 'it is strange that we should be willing to kill our own countrymen and commit a great sin.'

The conscientious scruples of the warrior Arjuna, which occupy most of the first chapter of the Gita, raise many questions. Arjuna queries not only fighting in general, although he was a soldier, but the ensuing fratricidal war since most of the combatants on both sides of the battle are related, and whatever happens will bring ruin to their race. Families will be broken up, women degraded, and virtue and laws abrogated. Arjuna was touched with compassion, he dropped his weapons and refused to fight, preferring like a pacifist to be killed rather than to kill.

It is not surprising that Marie Stopes's questions began at the opening of chapter two of the Gita. For here Krishna, the Lord God, with an enigmatic Mona Lisa smile, reprimanded Arjuna for folly and cowardice. Refusing to fight was a 'weakness which does no credit on those who call themselves Aryans.' Here and in later verses Krishna exhorted Arjuna to 'fight' and slay those who opposed him.

Various reasons were given for this belligerence: a soldier's duty, fear of cowardice, the indestructibility of the soul, and the killing action of God in which man is but a tool. It is not surprising that Marie Stopes put a double line and a large query against verse two. For the fact is that Krishna never answers Arjuna's plea for compassion, and on this point at least the Gita is cold and otherworldly. Although Gandhi preferred it on some points to the New Testament, the Gita is not a manual of pacifism but of renunciation of human ties and affections. So another question mark was placed against verse thirty-two which said that soldiers were lucky to find a battle and would go to heaven if they died in it.

In her unsuccessful first marriage, annulled as unconsummated, Marie Stopes became alarmed at the ignorant way in which European men and women embarked on married life, and she came to urge the importance of both passionate desire and planning of marital relations. Having begun the Gita with reverence, and having kept a book review which claimed that 'its power lies in shaping conduct in accordance with the needs of life', and presenting 'to the bewildered people of his age a synthetic view of the cosmos', she was surprised at its coldness. When the Gita continued (2, 62–64) that by desire 'reason is shattered', and that 'free from either attachment or repulsion he wins eternal peace', Marie Stopes burst out 'false and sterile'. And when the Gita maintained that 'desire breeds anger', she protested, 'no, very wrong—love'.

Throughout the Gita, whenever desire was condemned or detachment recommended, Marie Stopes scattered question marks. The Gita advocated impassivity: 'he looks impartially on all—lover, friend, or foe; indifferent or hostile; alien or relative; virtuous or sinful' (6, 9). She writes at the top of the page, 'a degraded teaching which has done much harm'. When the Gita praised action which was 'attended by no result, either good or bad' (9, 28), she asked, 'why so often this?' When the Gita said that the yogi 'neither likes nor dislikes', and 'loves friends and foes alike' (14, 24f.), Marie Stopes commented 'a poor and ineffective sort of goal'. What would she have thought of Plate 7 in Bhaktivedanta's *Gita as it is* on the verse 'the wise lament neither for the living nor the dead', and depicting a yogi walking calm and uncaring past a cripple, a mourner and a corpse?

The Gita urges detachment so that one is not swayed in action by hope of rewards or fears of punishment. Against those ascetics who tried to abandon all action, and so get free from contaminating karma, it declared that no one can remain without doing some action, even for a moment (3, 4–7). Indeed the ascetic who restrains his senses is likely to think about sensual things and is rightly called a hypocrite. The true way of action is to do one's duty, without any motive of gain, and, finally, to cast one's actions upon God for he will work in man.

Indian religion, or more especially Indian philosophy and ethics, has often been branded as world-renouncing, in contrast to the world-affirmation of Judaism, Islam and Christianity, the Indian religions differentiated thus from the Semitic. Nowadays there is a tendency to deny this contrast. Firstly, by noting world-renunciation in Christianity, with its monasteries and celibacy for religious specialists, and spirit against flesh and 'pie in the sky' for the masses. Secondly, by pointing out that Indian religions are much concerned with the present world. The culture which they inspired produced sensual sculptures that have few equals, and civilizations which were concerned with all aspects of social and personal life. Indian culture produced the Kama Sutra and many other books on sexual practices, which have been translated for the Islamic world and in modern times for the West.

God: Savage or Indifferent?

When I was giving the Wilde Lectures in Natural and Comparative Religion for three years in the university of Oxford, a great help and host was R. C. Zaehner, the Spalding Professor of Eastern Religions and Ethics. His rooms at All Souls College at that time were littered with galley proofs of his commentary on the Bhagavad Gita. Zaehner had translated the Gita at least twice, and though some of his renderings have been questioned there is little doubt that his work on the Gita is one of the most outstanding critical and exegetical commentaries on any non-Biblical religious book published this century.

There were discussions about some of the problems of the Gita and consideration of parallels in some of the Buddhist texts, with their similar teachings of indifference to friend and foe. Zaehner was critical of other modern translators of the Gita, especially President Radhakrishnan who was 'merely reading his own ideas into the text' by translating 'yoked' as 'union with the Divine'. Most pointedly he said that Radhakrishnan 'oscillates alarmingly between theism, pantheism and qualified monism because of his essentially indifferentist attitude to religion'. In this he was following Shankara, the classic monist or non-dualist, who could not interpret the Gita aright, because the relationship of love between God and man requires some distinction between them.

In his commentary of 1969, however, there was no sign of the outburst that came from Zaehner in his last book published in 1974. In that year of his premature death in Oxford came his strange work *Our Savage God*. The title indicates an attack on some Biblical statements about God, and its picture of what Zaehner called the 'savage, raving, raging, beserk God'. He seemed unable to discern progress or development in the Bible, for example between the bloody revolution of Jehu and the merciful teaching of Hosea who criticized him, or between the warrior Joshua and the peaceful Isaiah. Even the New Testament, said Zaehner, portrayed 'the same God', and he did not allow for the differences in men's understandings of God or the fact that all our knowledge is imperfect.

But most of this book is a devastating criticism of Indian teachings on the indifference and callousness of deity and saint alike. Since Zaehner was an expert on Indian classical language and theology, and had spent many years expounding Indian teachings, especially in the Gita, this was a strange turn round. Both his position and his publication gave far more open criticism of the Gita than was found in the notes of the personal copy which belonged to Marie Stopes.

Zaehner began *Our Savage God* by suggesting that some of the most horrible of recent murders might have been committed under the influence of Indian teachings of detachment from good and evil. An American professor had written to him hinting that the Manson murders of the actress Sharon Tate and five of her friends in 1969 could have been inspired, or at least justified, by the kind of detachment from human concerns and disregard for ordinary morality and rewards which appear to be taught in the Bhagavad Gita.

Zaehner did not clearly prove that there had been an influence of the Gita on Manson, but he hinted at the dangers of some of its teachings for morality in general. He suggested that 'one of the earliest scriptural texts that seems to justify Manson's philosophy of killing and being killed is found in the *Katha* Upanishad (2, 19):

> 'Should the killer think: "I kill",
> Or the killed: "I have been killed",
> Both these have no [right] knowledge:
> He does not kill nor is he killed.'

Zaehner continued, though it is not clear on what evidence, 'So too Charlie Manson draws his conclusions: "There is no good, there is no evil . . . You can't kill kill" and "If you're willing to be killed, you should be willing to kill". In terms of Indian religion this makes sense . . . if all things are ultimately One.'[1]

Zaehner does not say that the passage quoted is repeated almost word for word in the Bhagavad Gita (2, 19), and it provides one of its great texts for uncaring action, which is repeated again and again. Yet Zaehner had translated and commented on the Gita at great length, though in his standard verse by verse commentary his remarks on this passage are short and they simply refer back to the Katha Upanishad without

[1] *Our Savage God*, p. 47.

discussing the ethical value of the text. The moral, or immoral or amoral, implications of this verse seem to have simmered in his mind and boiled over in his last book.

This crucial verse might be expounded more, to show that Krishna did not answer Arjuna's problem of compassion, or tell him to turn the other cheek, but on the contrary Arjuna was urged to abandon his faintheartedness, pick up his arms and fight on as a warrior. At the end of the Gita the result of these long divine teachings is just that, carry on the battle. Krishna told Arjuna to perform his duty as a soldier, with no indication as to whether the cause was just or not. The principal teaching is that the soul is indestructible, never born and never dying. It is not slain when the body is slain. So the soldier who kills an enemy does not understand what he is doing, he can kill the body but he cannot kill the soul. The victim does not understand either, 'he thinks that he is slain', but he does not know that his soul is not killed. This might bring detachment to the soldier, like that expressed in Indian sculptures of most contorted sexual postures yet with calm and impassive faces. But it must be cold comfort for those who are being killed, and it shows a separation of flesh and spirit such as has also plagued Christianity in its world and marriage-renouncing aspects.

In defence of the Gita it can be claimed that it is not merely concerned with the battlefield, but it looks beyond to the whole of life. The very first word of the Gita is right-(*dharma*)-field, followed by Kuru-field where the battle took place; the whole scene is a pattern for human behaviour in all its aspects. The Gita commands action, not the renunciation of worldly duty or giving up daily work in ascetic resignation. Action must be performed for its own sake, simply because it is a duty, and not from hope of reward or fear of punishment, both of which can create cloying karma. Yet this activism and duty lead on to exhortations to consider friends and foes as the same and look beyond good and evil.

It has been questioned why the author of the Gita, who on any account was a distinguished poet, theologian and philosopher, should have chosen the warrior Arjuna to engage in this long discussion with the god Krishna. In previous chapters of the great epic Arjuna has appeared as handsome and brave but not conscience-striken. He fought against the god Shiva, and against many other warriors in single combat, and had various amorous adventures. Arjuna was much less thoughtful than his elder brother Yudhishthira, the 'king of righteousness', on whose behalf the whole struggle of the Indian epic was undertaken. But perhaps Arjuna was selected for the instructions of the Gita just because he represented the average man. He was not a Brahmin priest or an ascetic world–denier, and so the way of action, performance of god-given duty, without seeking rewards or honours, is held out as an ideal for this warrior and for all men. Men and women, high and low, for the Gita goes on to say that all people can come to God for help and find through him the way to salvation:

> 'All who come to me for refuge,
> even those whose birth is low,
> women, artisans, or serfs,
> upon the highest path shall go' (9, 32)

Avatar and Incarnation

In the Bhagavad Gita God speaks to man, and it is only one God. Both the divine voice and the divine unity are fresh in Hinduism, though later much of the worship of Shiva has been claimed as monotheistic. Perhaps there is a tendency towards unity in human thinking, and division or even opposition in the concepts of the godhead often came to seem inappropriate. Judaism insisted that 'the Lord our God, the Lord is one', and Islam insisted that 'there is no god but God'. Christianity developed the doctrine of the Trinity but maintained the unity, declaring that 'there is but one living and true God, without body, parts, or passions'.

Monotheism has been thought to be the property of the western or Semitic religions, but here it is in India, among the followers of Krishna, or those of Shiva. If the Buddha is a functional deity then a kind of monotheism is in south-east Asia also, and elsewhere people often hold to their particular divinity.

The Bhagavad Gita also teaches the involvement of God in the world, and in visible appearance 'whenever there is a decline of righteousness or rise of unrighteousness'. After this principle had been enunciated, although the word Avatar was not used, further Indian writings spoke of the Avatars, generally regarded as manifestations of the great god Vishnu. Rama was another great warrior-figure, a righteous Avatar whose story and worship have remained popular down to this day. Some listed ten Avatars, others twenty-two or more. Some of these were mythical beings, animals, half-human beings, or men. The Buddha himself was included among them, in efforts either to attract his followers or to discredit them.

The Avatar doctrines of Hinduism have been compared with the faith in the Incarnation in Christianity, and some writers like Aldous Huxley have maintained that 'the doctrine that God can be incarnated in human form' is found in most religions. In fact it is not found in some of the most important faiths, in Islam, or in Buddhism which goes beyond the gods, it is denied in Sikhism and unknown to the Zoroastrians. It is in Hinduism that ideas of Avatars flourished and where there are the closest parallels to Christianity. Yet Christian apologists have maintained that there is no real comparison, the Avatars were not human, not 'in flesh', or they merely 'drop into the human scene', without preparation in anything that has gone before in history. Some writers, however, have recognized that the Avatar is not docetic, a 'mere appearance', but a miracle in the human world brought about by the free will of God.

In the Wilde lectures on *Avatar and Incarnation* I distinguished twelve characteristics of Avatar doctrines that it seems can be fairly traced in the Gita and later Hindu texts, and it may be worth summarizing these in order to show Christian theologians what resemblances there may be between Christian and Hindu teachings.

1. The Avatar is real, in Hindu belief. It is a visible, and animal or human, descent of the divine to the mortal plane. It is either an incarnation or a theophany, and this appears most clearly in the two Avatars that still have millions of followers, Krishna and Rama.

2. Human Avatars are born of human parents who are named, and while there are infancy stories there are no parallels to the Virgin Birth.

3. The lives of the Avatars mingle human and divine powers; there are plenty of miracles, as there are also in the stories of the Buddha who was a real human person.

4. The Avatars finally die, Krishna by being wounded in the foot by Old Age, and Rama walking into a river which symbolized death.

5. Some Avatars may be historical. Both Krishna and Rama are regarded as historical figures in India, but as we have seen the stories of Krishna are complex and few critical historians would fix a date for his career or careers. Rama may have been a historical king, but again dates and details are uncertain.

6. Avatars are repeated. In the Gita Krishna says 'I come into being age after age'. It is the same deity who incarnates, in successive ages, and there have been both Avatars in the past and others to come. Kalki is the next promised eschatological Avatar, and the same notion of a coming figure is found in Buddhism.

7. The Avatars are important in character and example. While Krishna is many-sided, especially in the Puranas which delight

in his battles and amours, in the Gita he is noble, active and compassionate, and his disciple is told to follow his example. This is even more true of Rama, who is still held up as a pattern of a noble ruler and a faithful husband. His wife Sita is an example to wives of chastity and fidelity.

8.   The Avatar comes with a purpose. Avatars do not just come in the cycle of ages, but in response to need, 'whenever righteousness declines'.

9.   The Avatars show that the world is real. Much is made by critics of Indian other-worldliness and the *maya* or illusion of the world. But in the Gita the *maya* is the 'power' by which Krishna comes into the world. On this earth action is essential, and the harmony of society is fundamental.

10.   The Avatar is a revelation. It brings both words from God and his divine action. There are revelations from the gods in the scriptures, and a different revelation in the personal character of the Avatars.

11.   The Avatars reveal a personal God. The Upanishads seek the impersonal, That, and go as far as they can in getting rid of symbolism or too-human notions of the divine. But men need a personal God in devotion and Krishna is revealed as the Highest Being, the Manifest beyond the Unmanifest.

12.   Avatars reveal a God of grace. Krishna is called the Friend of all beings, he is implored to show forgiveness, to be not only as father to son but as lover to beloved (11, 44). As the devotee is 'very dear' to God, so he is 'exceedingly beloved' by God.

There have been critics in India of the Avatar doctrines, as unnecessary or contradictory, or too limiting to the nature of God. But the Gita declares:

'Foolish men hold me in scorn
when I take a human form,
knowing not my higher being
as the mighty Lord of beings'. (9, 11)

69

Chapter Seven

SIKH SYNTHESIS?

Concrete Pyramid

In 1969 the fifth centenary of the birth of Guru Nanak, founder of the Sikh religion, was celebrated in India and other countries. A notable public meeting was in the Albert Hall, London, and among the guests really was the Archbishop of Canterbury. In India an International Seminar on Guru Nanak's Life and Thought was held at the University of the Punjab at Patiala. I was invited to attend, with two other scholars from Britain, others from Europe and America, and large numbers from India.

The Punjabi university at Patiala was founded in 1962 and five years later there was inaugurated a Guru Gobind Singh department of Religious Studies, so named after the third centenary of the birth of the tenth Guru of the Sikhs. This was the first department of Comparative Religion in an Indian university, and it may seem strange that a country with such rich and varied religious traditions should previously have seemed unwilling to make religion a subject of academic study. But independent India had a policy of what is called 'secularism', not in the European sense of irreligion but in the local meaning of impartiality between religions. There is a Hindu university at Benares (Varanasi), where Sanskrit language and philosophy have been taught, the latter usually in English, but until recently it had no department of religious studies as such. Other Indian universities had lectureships in philosophy, but Patiala was the first to launch into fullscale religious studies.

The Sikhs were well placed for inter-religious courses, because it has long been thought that the Sikh religion stands somewhere between Hinduism and Islam, if indeed it is not a synthesis of some elements of each of them. Sikhism is also a monotheism, like Islam, Judaism and Christianity, though it has grown up amid a polytheistic Hindu environment. The new department of Religious Studies at Patiala had been planned with five sections, each in charge of an expert in the relevant discipline, dedicated to the 'five religions' that seemed to be of most concern to India: Buddhism, Christianity, Hinduism, Islam, and Sikhism.

To house this department a monumental building had been conceived, the Guru Gobind Singh Bhavan, which was formally opened during the conference. The Bhavan, a centre, meeting or 'being-place', is a great concrete and glass pyramid, designed by the university architect and built at considerable cost. It has five lower sections, representing five lotus petals, a sacred Indian flower, stretched out over a pool of water which surrounds the building. Here libraries are housed, with rooms for study and meditation in each of the religions, and other petals could be added for other religions. From these petals rise five arches, joining in a glass dome at a height of thirty metres, with the whole crowned by an electric perpetual flame to symbolize the eternity of the soul. It is proposed to cover the whole Bhavan eventually with white marble, at further high expense.

Klaus Klostermaier, in the account of his stay at the Krishna pilgrimage centre at Vrindaban (p. 50 above), remarked on the difference between theology at 70 degrees Fahrenheit and theology at 120 degrees. In a European seminary at 70 degrees it was easy to think of God as impassive, and of the world as a beautiful harmony, with evil simply regarded as the absence of good or the shadow of the light. But at 120 degrees at Vrindaban the theologian had to take into account the reality of human suffering, the fact of evil, and the effect of this upon human conceptions of God.

Architecture may have a similar effect according to temperate or tropical climates, and modernistic concrete and glass which may be appropriate to Scandinavia are unlikely to help calm discussion near the equator. In the past, India experimented with many kinds of building styles, seeking to combine elegance with coolness, and one of these might have provided a better model for the Bhavan even if it was traditional. Some of the conference delegates had just come from Delhi and had visited the Red Fort with its gracious pavilions. The Diwan-i-Khas, the Hall of Private Audience there, was built of white marble but it had fretted screens, no glass, and it was open to the wind on all sides. In the days of the Mogul empire cooling streams ran right through this hall, and above the arches at either end of the pavilion there are inscriptions in Persian:

> If there is a Paradise on earth,
> it is this,
> oh! it is this!
> oh! it is this!

But at Patiala the great panes of glass in the Bhavan magnified the sun's rays. To counteract the heat scores of fans were brought in, but their noise made hearing the lectures difficult. A loudspeaker system worked erratically and it had to combat echoes coming back from the concrete walls. The concrete shell also retained the heat long after the sun had set. The monsoon had just ended, and the damp heat was stifling, so that theological discussion at 120 degrees added problems to differences of opinions. To increase diversions, pigeons soon found a way into the Bhavan through doors and windows, and on ledges high up inside the five wings they found rubble and dust left by the builders, and distributed them impartially on the heads of scholars sitting sweating below. The water surrounding the Bhavan should have helped coolness, but it was unsuitable for drinking, and relays of servants with glasses of water on trays constantly passed between the conference benches.

Ghost at the Feast

Such distractions amid the heat did not minimize the importance of a seminar which brought together Sikh and Hindu, Muslim and Christian scholars, to discuss some of the religious and philosophical themes of Sikhism. They seemed to agree that Guru Nanak was a holy man and an outstanding teacher, developing doctrines of one God and his relations with men, such as might be found in contemporary Hindu movements and in Islam, though he presented original teachings to his Sikhs, his 'disciples'.

It soon appeared, however, that interpretation of Sikh doctrines could vary according to the viewpoint of the speaker. Thus for a Hindu philospher, 'Nanak is not only a monist but also a pantheist. He stresses the unity of the creator and the creation. He holds that the Lord is himself the enjoyer, the enjoyment and the enjoyed, the lover and the beloved, the fish, the water, the net and the weight.' And another Hindu affirmed that 'the Guru has directly realized the Absolute, he is the Absolute incarnate.'

Direct contradiction of the pantheistic interpretation of Sikhism came, not unnaturally, from a Muslim who said that 'the whole tenor of Nanak's thought about God is completely opposed to the Vedantic view of which Shankara was the chief exponent'. So Nanak's concept of God was 'essentially Islamic... It is often forgotten that the formative years of Nanak's life were passed in a land whose towns and villages were honeycombed with Muslim saints and faqirs.'

Among Sikhs themselves there were apparent tendencies towards both personalistic and monistic ideas of the divine, and also some emphasis on Sikhism as a synthesis of religious thought. One Sikh scholar, Singh Kohli, affirmed that the very first words of the Sikh daily prayer, 'There is one God' conveys 'the unity of Brahman and also its two aspects, namely, the unmanifested and the manifested.' Guru Nanak, he said, discarded all other symbols, Hindu names for God and his Avatars, and 'considered Brahman's name as mere outward symbol and the only mode of contact with him.' Further, 'all the gods or Avataras (incarnations) are created by Brahman, and therefore they are not to be considered as Brahman.'

For European and American scholars a gift had seemed to come from heaven shortly before this conference, in the publication of a critical study of Sikh history and doctrine by W. H. McLeod in *Guru Nānak and the Sikh Religion*. Dr McLeod had been teaching in a missionary college in India but, like some other missionaries, he had become absorbed in the study of another religion, in his case Sikhism, and had become an expert in the Punjabi language, studying at firsthand the sacred texts and legends of the Sikh religion. His long and detailed book had earned him a doctorate in philosophy at the university of London, and it was published by Clarendon Press in Oxford.

But it was the ghost at the feast. An exhibition was held in the Patiala university library of classical Sikh manuscripts in the Punjabi language, and copies of books were on display which were said to represent all the works on Sikhism in foreign languages. McLeod's book was hot from the press, too hot to handle, and it was not there.

Some overseas visitors had got up their Sikhism from McLeod's book, and one American lecture was largely an exposition of McLeod, comparing his work on Sikh texts with the 'demythologizing' school which applied critical study to the Bible. But to most Sikhs the searching analytical method of the book had come as a shock, and some denounced it openly, while others pointed out the alien character of such critical treatment of religious texts in the Indian environment. It was one thing to admit, as an eminent Sikh scholar had done in writing, that the stories and biographies of Guru Nanak were sometimes crude or badly expressed. It was quite different to dismiss nearly all such stories, as McLeod had done, so that his outline of the life of Guru Nanak occupied less than one page in his long book.

Even now, years later, McLeod's book is not generally acceptable to Sikhs. Since he was a Christian missionary, some have suggested that his motive in critically under-mining traditions was to destroy Sikhism, although his book showed no attempt at conversion and he ended by praising 'the combination of piety and practical activity' which Guru Nanak showed in his own life and bequeathed to his followers.

Some non-Sikh scholars have said that McLeod's stringent analysis raises the question of the value to be attached to legend and myth in religious study. It used to be fashionable in academic circles to dismiss all extraordinary events, let alone miracles, in any scriptures as later additions or mere superstition. But now it is recognized that myth and miracle both need to be studied in order to gain understanding of a religion. At least they show what believers hold about their faith, and this fact should be given proper weight. To dismiss myth from religion would be like dismissing poetry from literature, a fatal impoverishment in either case. In some ways, it was suggested, McLeod's rejection of the legendary and mythical was rather old-fashioned, and more rather than less room should be given to them in order to facilitate understanding of Sikh religion and history.

The Gurus
Nanak, the first of the Sikh Gurus, 'teachers' or spiritual preceptors, was born in 1469 at Talwandi about fifty miles west of Lahore in what is now Pakistan. This is Panjab ('five' tributaries of the river Indus) in the north-west of the sub-continent and most of the inhabitants at the time were Hindus.

There were important pilgrimage centres for worshippers of Shiva and Krishna among others, and devotional worship (*bhakti*) was expressed in the singing of hymns which the Sikhs adopted in congregational praise. Islam had entered India several centuries before and Sufis, Islamic mystics, had won many converts among the Hindus who regarded them as Gurus. There were also individual holy men and women, such as Kabir, who looked beyond the differences of Hindus and Muslims to teach faith in one God.

Nanak was born into a mercantile caste family and his father was a Hindu who collected revenue for the Muslim owner of his village. He married a woman of a related caste group and his wife bore him two sons. He worked in the town of Sultanpur as steward to an Afghan administrator. There are legends of Nanak's childhood and when he was thirty years of age he had an experience of enlightenment. It is said that Nanak went to bathe ritually in a river and failed to return, his clothes being found on the bank. There was great concern, the river was dragged and it was assumed that he had drowned.

After three days Nanak returned and eventually declared, 'There is neither Hindu nor Muslim, so whose path shall I follow? God is neither Hindu nor Muslim, so I shall follow God's path.' He then revealed that he had been taken to the court of God and given a cup of nectar (*amrit*) and told, 'This is the cup of the adoration of the Name of God. Drink it. I am with you, Go, rejoice in my Name and teach others to do so.'

Following this experience Nanak uttered the Mool Mantra, 'basic text', a confession of faith and basic theological statement, with which the Sikh scriptures, the Adi Granth, opens and which is used in Sikh daily prayer:

> 'There is one God,
> his Name is eternal truth,
> Creator of all things and pervading all,
> without fear or enmity,

timeless and formless,
beyond birth and death,
manifesting himself,
known by the grace of the Guru.'

In response to his divine vocation Nanak began to travel
about India and perhaps beyond. It seems that he visited
important centres of pilgrimage of both Hindus and Muslims,
and engaged in debate with Yogis and other religious leaders.
There are many legends of the travels recorded in *janam-sakhis*,
traditional biographies which were compiled up to a hundred
years after the death of Nanak. He is said to have visited the
great temple complex at Puri on the eastern coast of India where
Krishna is worshipped as 'world-lord' (Jagannatha,
Juggernaut). In the other direction he is believed to have
travelled as far as western Arabia where Muslims make the
pilgrimage to Mecca. Critical scholars reject most of such tales,
while admitting that they may represent visits to nearer temples
and pilgrimage sites. But the legends do present a picture of the
veneration accorded to Nanak, and belief in the originality and
universality of his mission, as seen by early Sikhs.

Perhaps it was after most of his journeyings that a wealthy
follower gave Nanak and his disciples some land on the banks of
the Ravi, a tributary of the Indus river, and the village of
Kartarpur was built where Nanak spent the rest of his days. He
visited nearby places, engaged in debates, and attracted many
disciples. The Guru died at Kartarpur in 1539 at the age of
seventy.

Fundamental to Sikhism is the role of the Guru and before he
died Nanak appointed a devout and able successor, Angad, to
lead the community in preference to either of his sons. There
were ten Gurus in all, the third, Amar Das, organized the
community and instituted the traditions of langars or free
kitchens wherein Sikhs and visitors are given hospitality. The
fourth Guru, Ram Das, founded the city of Amritsar, 'pool of

77

nectar', on a site given by the tolerant Mogul emperor Akbar, and the city remains the centre of Sikh organization. His son, Guru Arjan, both built the place of worship where the famous Golden Temple now stands, and produced the first collection of scriptures containing hymns of the Gurus and of some Hindu and Muslim saints.

The emperor Akbar was followed by less tolerant rulers and his great grandson Aurangzeb, who ruled for nearly fifty years (till 1707), was a fanatical Muslim who imposed forcible conversions, demolished temples and images, and persecuted Hindus and Sikhs alike. The tenth Sikh Guru, Gobind Singh (1666–1708), founded a militant inner brotherhood called the Khalsa, 'pure ones'. Members were initiated with water stirred with a two-edged sword. They were to wear five symbols (five K's in the Punjabi language): hair and beard uncut, a steel comb, steel bangle on the right wrist, a short sword, and short breeches. Initiated men were given the name Singh, 'lion', and women were called Kaur, 'princess'.

The succession of ten human Gurus came to an end with Gobind Singh, and he indicated the scripture as his successor so that it is known as Guru Granth Sahib, 'teacher-book-lord', as well as Adi Granth, 'original book'. The Gurus have been regarded as perfect, sinless, models of devotion. Each Guru was held to be identical in essence with his predecessors, and they all signed themselves Nanak. The Guru was said to 'live within his Sikhs', or the Sikh was held to 'incorporate his Guru'. Similarly with the scripture, 'the Guru is the Word and the Word is the Guru'. So that to Sikhs the Gurus were not just reformers, or uniters of the best in Hinduism and Islam, but they were perfect and exalted. Sikh prayers begin with the invocation of God and the Guru, and are punctuated with exclamations of 'Wonderful Lord'. It is said that the Guru is identified with the voice of God, with the means whereby God imparts truth. How close is this to the Word made flesh?

Golden Temple

The Golden Temple of Amritsar is called Hari Mandir, 'temple of the Lord' or Darbar Sahib, 'divine court'. It is a white building with golden domes, standing in the middle of an artificial lake, in which visitors wash themselves ritually as they do in the lakes and tanks of Hindu temples. The lake is surrounded on four sides by black and white marble pavements, and at intervals there are shrines of Sikh martyrs where flowers are regularly laid. In the temple there are inlays of semi-precious stones and mirrors. There are gilded verses from the scriptures on the walls, and murals of scenes from the life of Guru Nanak, but no images.

Early every morning the Sikh scriptures are carried from a treasury in a silver ark by a procession of men, while trumpeters blow on horns, somewhat like the Jewish procession of the Torah. The ark is taken along a causeway into the temple, and there all day long it is read in a plainchant by a succession of bearded elders. Worshippers come to bow and go round the shrine where the scriptures are being read, receiving in return for their gifts portions of sweetmeat, the Prasad or offering made to the deity and shared by the worshippers like a communion meal.

There are many other temples and holy places. At Tarn Taran, fifteen miles from Amritsar, is a fine temple of the fifth Guru, the walls decorated with scenes from the lives of saints and pictures of animals and birds. Wherever there are Sikhs there is a Gurdwara, a place where there is a copy of the Guru Granth Sahib. It is marked by a yellow Sikh flag, though its size may vary from an ornate white temple to a small flat-roofed building, or abroad a house in a terrace.

The third Guru built a place of pilgrimage at Goindwal, where eighty-four steps lead down to a tank or well, the number of steps corresponding to the number of rebirths in the Hindu cycle of existence. Pilgrims go down one side of the steps and come up on the other, seeking by this visit and recitation of texts to reduce or abolish the number of rebirths. Here, although the scriptures denounce the Hindu belief in Avatars, there are wall pictures of the Fish and Tortoise Avatars of Vishnu.

In the struggles of the Sikhs against persecution the Golden Temple and other shrines suffered desecration, followed by restoration. The latest struggle came in 1984 when on 6 June the Golden Temple was stormed by the Indian army. There had long been struggles for Sikh political independence, and the most determined had seized the Golden Temple as a centre for operations to set up a separate Sikh state. Although many Sikhs did not agree with the extremists, the governmental seizure of their most holy shrine, with the death of many Sikhs, shocked even the most tolerant and probably decisively changed attitudes of accommodation with other Indian religions.

Synthesis or Separation?
One virtue of McLeod's, which was more easily accepted by Sikhs than his onslaught on legend, was a long statement and exposition of the teachings of Guru Nanak. The Guru's life might fill less than a page, but his doctrines were detailed in nearly eighty pages of McLeod. Here was the systematic presentation that one looked for in vain elsewhere since a well-known Sikh, Trilochan Singh, had admitted that many works on the teachings were written with 'extremely superficial and crudely grasped and digested knowledge of the concepts', and were 'extremely disappointing'. He declared that 'there is no such thing as dogmatic theology in Sikhism', but this is all to the good since theology, he claimed, tends to sacrifice the larger interests of religion to creed and uniformity.

McLeod investigated early Sikh ideas of the nature of the divine, saying, 'as in the case of Kabīr monistic language does indeed occur, but the structure of monistic thought can provide no place for Guru Nānak's concept of God.' It was different from Hindu thought, both in the monism of the Vedanta and the Avatar doctrines of the Vishnu cults. For Nanak, God is unborn and not incarnated. He is beyond death and transmigration, and 'this, by implication, means that there can be no place for a doctrine of avatārs.'[1]

On the other hand Sikhism did not just take over the idea of a single transcendent God from Islam. McLeod points out that there were many monotheistic movements within Hinduism, from the Bhagavad Gita to Kabir. Nanak was not just an isolated figure, or a deliberate synthesizer, but his own original religious experiences framed the doctrines and the religion.

Yet some Sikhs have maintained that their religion is a deliberate mixture of ideas, and have held that this gives Sikhism a special place in the modern world where religions are meeting as never before. Sohan Singh declares that 'Sikhism attempts to effect a synthesis of the two streams of religious consciousness', the Indian and the Semitic. Could this not be a special reason for the appeal of Sikhism today, among the multiplicity of religions in the modern world revealing a religion that combines the best in the two major traditions of religion?

On the other hand there are some who have maintained that Sikhism should merge into Hinduism, which is held to be an all-inclusive religion. In 1953 the well-known author and journalist Khushwant Singh caused dismay when he ended his book *The Sikhs* by remarking that the lessening of Hindu-Sikh conflict 'has increased the tempo of Sikh merger into Hinduism.' He thought that at the present pace 'there is little doubt that before the century has run its course Sikh religion will have become a branch of Hinduism and the Sikhs a part of the Hindu social system.' He suggested that Guru Nanak was a reformer rather

[1] *Gurū Nānak and the Sikh Religion*, p. 146ff.

than a deliberate founder of a new religion, but that the formation of the Sikh scriptures, the resistance of Sikhs to Mogul persecution, and the invention of the Khalsa brotherhood by Gobind Singh had marked Sikhism off as a separate religion. Some writers have said much the same of the origins of Christianity, but the fact remains that it developed as a distinctive religion.

Sikhs are notable by their dress, with beard uncut and hair covered with a turban. But Khushwant Singh pointed out that many Sikhs no longer observed the rules strictly. 'With the Sikh upper classes trimming of beards and smoking is not uncommon. Among the Sikh peasantry the position is much worse. . . . The only class of Sikhs to observe strictly the forms and symbols of Sikhism are the lower middle-class from northern Punjab.'

There was strong opposition to such views, even before the traumatic events of 1984. Leaders like Teja Singh held firmly that Sikhism must remain distinctive, and it should launch a missionary movement to increase its numbers among other races and classes than the Punjabis. McLeod also considered that Sikhism has been saved from absorption into Hinduism by its distinctive features, its particular scripture and recognizable insignia, especially beard and turban, and that these will continue.

Then there have been those who have been as dogmatic as the exclusivist proponents of other religions. At the conference at Patiala, which was intended to bring appreciations of Guru Nanak from both Sikhs and members of other religions, an anonymous writer circulated a fiery pamphlet. This declared that Sikhism is the only true religion, so that discussion with other religions is useless and treasonable.

The invasion of the Golden Temple at Amritsar by Indian troops in 1984, with the loss of many Sikh lives, shocked not only extremist Sikhs but the whole community, including the liberal elements. Khushwant Singh himself spoke publicly of his dismay and horror at this desecration, and whatever 'lessening' there may have been of Hindu–Sikh conflict thirty years ago this was now reversed. When Mrs Gandhi was assassinated by Sikhs towards the end of that year, Hindu mobs took their revenge on Sikhs and hundreds were killed. Whatever the future may hold there will be tension for a long time, and the Sikh community will maintain its distinctiveness.

A further feature, as with some other eastern religions, is the Dispersion abroad. There are large Sikh communities overseas, formerly in East Africa and now in Britain. These are affected by the societies into which they go, and in turn the Dispersion will affect those who remain in the homeland. Tendencies towards absorption in the Dispersion may be halted, for a time at least, by the resurgence of Sikh religious and communal convictions.

Chapter Eight

PROPHET OF ISLAM

Muhammad the Man
Driving from the Samaritan town of Nablus discussion was
attempted on the religions: Samaritan and Jewish, Muslim and
Christian. I asked my Arab companion what he thought of
Christ and was countered by his demanding an opinion of
Muhammad. Was he a prophet? Unless this question were
answered there could be no discussion, and it applies on a larger
scale to the whole Islamic world.

Christian 'recognition' of Muhammad has for long been a
concern and a demand by Muslims in conversations. When
attempts are made, as they have been increasingly in this
century, for 'dialogue' between religions, the first question of
Muslims has been 'why do you not acknowledge our Prophet?'
Christians have often been hesitant, because of their past history
and because of the supposed theological implications of the
question. But it is a question that must be answered.

No great religious leader has been so maligned and
misrepresented, outside his religion, and Christian attitudes
towards him have been lamentable. Even now, when non-
Muslim writings about Islam may be factual and fairly accurate,
there is little understanding by scholars of the religious
importance of Muhammad for the believer. Yet this Prophet
was undoubtedly one of the most influential teachers of
mankind, the religion of Islam has formed great civilizations,
the Muslim world is powerful today with the second largest
membership of any religion, and Muslim communities are
found in many western countries.

In the Middle Ages Muslims were lampooned as worshipping
idols called Baphomet (Mahomet, the old spelling), which they

never did being the most firm rejecters of all forms of idolatry. Muhammad was said in Christian propaganda to have trained a pigeon to pick peas out of his ear, which was explained as the Holy Spirit supposedly talking to him. Dante in his *Divine Comedy* put Muhammad in the Ninth Chasm of Hell, with his body mangled because he had been a 'sower of scandal and schism'. Yet the Muslim warrior Saladin, who was respected by the Crusaders and the Islamic philosophers Avicenna and Averroes were put with Socrates, Plato and Aristotle among the virtuous pagans in the first circle, in Limbo above the pangs of Hell. Even the reformer Zwingli, who thought that Socrates and Hercules might be in heaven, called Muhammad a blind leader of the blind and a slave of sensual passions. Nineteenth century missionary writers called Muhammad the Great Impostor, and even in this century he has been termed a False Prophet.

That Muhammad was a sensual man, apparently a shocking trait in a prophet, has been a constant theme of critical attack. Hebrew heroes might be excused for gross sexuality, like King David who not only lusted after another man's wife but sent Uriah to death in order to gain Bath-sheba, and Solomon whose many wives and concubines led him astray from God. But Muhammad has not been so excused, or understood, and a modern German scholar repeats the charge that Muhammad was a sensual man who surrounded himself with young women.

No one denies that Muhammad had a number of wives, but what were the circumstances? This supposedly sensual man was not married till he was twenty-five. Then he married Khadija, a widow of forty who had been married twice before, and they lived together in fidelity for the next twenty-four years. Khadija bore Muhammad all but one of his eight children, and only after her death did he take another wife, another widow, when he was fifty.

Muhammad died when he was sixty-two, and in the last

twelve years of his life he had some fourteen wives and concubines. Only one of these women was a virgin, Ayesha, daughter of his chief follower and the first caliph, Abu Bakr. Muhammad married the daughter of his second chief follower, Omar, and this man strengthened the family ties by himself marrying Muhammad's granddaughter. The third caliph-to-be, married two of Muhammad's daughters, and the fourth, Ali, married his daughter Fatima. Four years before his death Muhammad took a Coptic concubine, Mariyah or Mary, who had been presented to him by the Christian ruler of Egypt, and she bore him a son but the child soon died to the great grief of the parents.

This undoubted polygamy must be seen in the context of the time and the development of Muhammad's religious movement. The polygamy of Old Testament heroes, Abraham and Jacob among others, is well known and it was standard practice for anyone of importance. Even Hebrew priests sometimes had more than one wife, and marriage was regarded as instituted and blessed by God and not to be renounced. To 'be fruitful and multiply and replenish the earth' was a religious command, for the family as well as in agriculture. In ancient Arab society, as in many others, plural marriages had the principal aim of maintaining the population as well as showing the importance of the patriarch.

Some of Muhammad's wives were taken to give them protection after they had become widows, and others were married for dynastic reasons, to strengthen ties with some of his chief followers and to provide heirs for a succession. In the latter aim he was unfortunate, since all his sons died young and of the daughters only Fatima survived her father by a year. Muhammad was less lucky than Henry VIII in seeking sons and daughters by multiple marriages, but he was more kindly than that Sovereign Lord of the Church of England, since he cared for his wives and divorced or executed none of them.

An eminent Christian scholar, after a careful study of these marriages, remarks that 'it is not too much to say that *all* Muhammad's marriages had a political aspect.'[1] Modern Muslim writers go further, claiming that Muhammad as a married man and a father, as well as ruler and warrior, gave a model of life for the ordinary believer. He knew the needs and cares of family life, and gave a pattern of fatherhood, husbandly care, and religion. Far from renouncing the world with its toils and struggles, like some ascetic religious teachers, Muhammad lived in the world and yet he was a man devoted to God.

Thomas Carlyle wrote an essay on 'The Hero as Prophet', in *Heroes and Hero-Worship*, in the last century. He was one of the first Europeans to recognize the moral stature of Muhammad, and his writing has been appreciated in the Islamic world. He said, 'Mahomet himself, after all that can be said of him, was not a sensual man... His household was of the frugalest; his common diet barley-bread and water: sometimes for months there was not a fire once lighted on his hearth. They record with just pride that he would mend his own shoes, patch his own cloak.' Islam, like many religious movements in their beginnings, was puritanical. 'His religion was not an easy one: with rigorous fasts, lavations, strict complex formulas, prayers five times a day, and abstinence from wine, it did not "succeed by being an easy religion". As if indeed any religion, or cause holding of religion, could succeed by that!'

Holy War

That Islam was spread by the sword, with the cry 'Believe or perish' to its opponents, is one of the commonest criticisms of Muhammad and his religion, and again the facts must be considered in context. Until A.D. 622, when he was fifty-two, Muhammad lived at Mecca, his birthplace, with a growing

[1] W. M. Watt, *Muhammad at Medina*, 1956, p. 330ff.

band of followers. There had been opposition to their rejection of idols and faith in only one God, and some took refuge in Christian Ethiopia. The rulers of Mecca feared that the message of one God would undermine both their polytheistic religion and their authority, and eventually Muhammad himself migrated to Medina. This was a group of settlements two hundred miles to the north, and he stayed there for the last ten years of his life. This Migration was the Hijra (or Hegira) from which Islamic history is dated.

From this stronger position, which commanded the trade routes to Mecca, and where Muhammad was a dominant figure, it was almost inevitable that there would be conflict with the Meccans. Muhammad's followers needed economic support and under his leadership they intercepted a caravan returning to Mecca from Syria. Warriors were sent from Mecca to help and the Muslims were outnumbered by three to one, yet they had a complete victory at the battle of Badr in 624 which became an important milestone in the development of the community. The following year the Meccans attacked Medina with an even larger force and wounded the Prophet, but withdrew after a token victory. After a final attack, the community at Medina was left in peace and in 630 Muhammad returned in triumph to Mecca, which submitted with little opposition. This was called 'the farewell pilgrimage', since he was soon taken ill and died at Medina in the arms of Ayesha.

The Koran speaks first of defensive fighting, 'fight in the way of God against those who fight against you, but do not be aggressors' (2, 186), and later, 'fighting is a grave offence, but hindering men from the way of God . . . is graver still' (2, 214). Jihad, 'holy war', meant originally 'striving', as Muslims were told to 'strive in the way of religion'. In time the Jihad became the action of the religious community against non-believers, especially idolaters. In Muslim wars the unbelievers, 'kafirs', were told to submit or perish, but the 'People of the Book', especially Jews and Christians, were allowed to continue in their religions as recognized religious minorities.

Muslim justifications of the Jihad are similar in some respects to doctrines of the Just War, with which other religions have wrestled. First, there is the question of what would have happened if the young Muslim community had not either defended itself, or attacked when opportunity offered, though such speculations may be unimportant since the fights took place and it is assumed that they were in the will of God. A rare suggestion comes from a modern Egyptian writer, Dr Kamel Hussein, who says, 'Had the Muslims let their Prophet die at the hands of the Quraish without striking a blow for his safety, the history of Islam would probably have been identical with the history of Christianity, growing through submission, humility and heroic resistance to persecution.'[2]

But there is the further question of the relation of religion to the state, and Islam has not divided the two. Political power has gone along with religious dominance. Islam was a success religion from the start, at least from the battle of Badr, and was in sharp contrast to Christianity which was persecuted for the first three centuries. Eventually Christianity triumphed, sometimes dominating the state, sometimes being dominated. To this day there are some Christian states with established churches—but that is another story, and the development of Islam was different.

The great Islamic historian Ibn Khaldun, from fourteenth century Spain, wrote of the importance of righteous anger and action in the service of God: 'if the power of wrathfulness were no longer to exist in man, he would lose the ability to help the truth become victorious. Then there would no longer be Jihad, or glorification of the word of God.' He contrasted the missionary Jihad of Islam with Christianity which, he thought,

---

[2] *City of Wrong*, English translation 1959, p. 224.

was not really a 'missionary religion' because it did not use power to back up its message, and so it had no competence to establish a just society.

Such joining faith with power, religion and politics, was amply demonstrated in the early and rapid extension of Islam. It was the most immediately successful of all the world's religions. Muhammad died in 632 and in just a hundred years the Arab armies overran Syria, Mesopotamia, Persia, entered India and sent envoys to China. While in the west north Africa was conquered, Spain crossed, and the advance was only checked by the armies of Charles Martel, at Poitiers in the heart of France in 732.

This was Arab expansion and imperialism, defeating the old Christian empire of Constantinople up to the borders of the great city itself, and taking over the Zoroastrian empire of Persia. Conversion to Islam was not imposed on monotheistic populations, though preachers followed the armies and there was social pressure to conform to Islam in the ensuing centuries.

Most of the Christian churches in the Middle East were Monophysite or Syrian, whose doctrines differed from the 'orthodox' of Constantinople who often ruled them oppressively. They were not averse to a change of masters, and it was the Christian patriarch of Jerusalem who opened the city gates to the Arabs. He showed the Caliph Omar round the city, noting his shabby clothes, and securing respect for the Church of the Holy Sepulchre. The so-called 'mosque of Omar', or Dome of the Rock, was eventually built on the site of the old temple, cleared of Roman ruins, largely erected by Christian craftsmen and remaining to this day.

Similarly the Christian patriarch of Alexandria opened the city gates to the Arabs, this finest city in the western world after Constantinople being taken in peace on payment of tribute and guarantee of protection from recovery by the Byzantines. The Muslims respected the churches and an old story, still repeated in the West, that the Arabs destroyed the ancient library of Alexandria under the pretext that all wisdom is in the Koran, is a complete libel. Two earlier libraries had been destroyed there by Julius Caesar and the emperor Theodosius, and when the Arabs arrived there was no library of importance in Alexandria. The fairy tale of this library destruction did not appear till six hundred years later, mentioned by a Mesopotamian polemicist.

A more serious criticism of Muhammad than the use of warfare has been the treatment of the three Jewish communities that were in Medina when he arrived there. Rightly or wrongly they were suspected of complicity with the attacking Meccans, and no doubt the latter would have looked for allies and disaffected elements in Medina. After the first Muslim-Meccan battle, one Jewish tribe was expelled from Medina, and a second after the next siege. Two years later, after the failure of a large Meccan onslaught, the remaining Medinan Jews, the Qurayzah, were accused of treachery, 'siding with the confederates'. They surrendered unconditionally and Muhammad passed the judgement on their fate over to a clan leader who had been wounded in the skirmishes. He decreed that all the men should be killed, and the women and children enslaved. This was done and some six hundred men were said to have been slaughtered.

It was a bloody act, and it is not to excuse but put it in context that it should be stated that it was done under stress of war and accusations of treason, that the clan had no bonds of loyalty to the Muslims, or they to them, and that it was a community decision. The early historians show no compunction about such actions, but an Indian Muslim has argued recently that the executions took place on the field of battle, in the heat of conflict, and that the numbers have been greatly exaggerated.

Again it is not an excuse but a reminder, to recall that many other politico-religious leaders have been responsible for similar bloody actions, from Moses and David to the Crusaders and Cortes. Despite the unhappy fate of the Jews of Medina,

Judaism was respected by Muhammad, its prophets were revered and many of them named in the Koran, and in general Jews fared better under later Islam than under medieval Christianity. The modern quarrels of the Arabs with the state of Israel are political, and Muslim leaders have distinguished between Judaism and Zionism.

Love of the prophet

Muslims affirm that Muhammad was a man, and he performed no miracles, though there are traditional stories of miracles and wonders connected with him. But the great miracle was the Koran, the Word of God brought to men.

The Shahada, the 'witness' of Islam to the unity of God, the first of the Pillars of religion, which is recited many times every day, says:

> I bear witness that there is no god but God,
> and I bear witness that Muhammad is the Apostle
> of God.

Muhammad was a prophet and messenger or apostle of God, in the succession of the prophets and apostles of the Bible. But for the Muslim world Muhammad is far more than that. He is not simply *a* prophet, but *the* prophet. The Koran calls him 'the Seal of the Prophets', perhaps in the sense of one who confirms and seals up the prophecies that had gone before, making them all plain, but this is taken to mean that he was the last and greatest prophet, after whom there can be no other prophet.

Muhammad is believed to have been sinless, as all prophets were according to Islamic tradition. He has been called 'second only to God', and in mosques his name is often alongside that of Allah on the wall which worshippers face. Muhammad is not worshipped, strictly, but he is more than venerated or revered.

Constance Padwick, a Christian missionary, spent many

years studying popular prayer-books which are found on sale in shops right across the Islamic world, from Algiers to Baghdad, and from Istanbul to Omdurman and Bombay. Her findings were published in *Muslim Devotions*, and revealed a world of devotion in some ways unique and in other ways similar to the prayers of other religions. One important element that she revealed, which critical scholars of Islam often neglect, is the importance of Muhammad in devotion. It is not enough to study the historical and the political in Islam, there is also the devotional and mystical.

'No one,' wrote Miss Padwick, 'can estimate the power of Islam as a religion who does not take into account the love at the heart of it for this figure [Muhammad]. It is here that human emotion, repressed at some points by the austerity of the doctrine of God as developed in theology, has its full outlet—a warm human emotion which the peasant can share with the mystic. The love of this figure is perhaps the strongest binding force in a religion which has so marked a binding power.'[3]

One of the commonest phrases on Muslim lips is the blessing of peace: 'May God call down blessing on our Lord Muhammad, and on the family of our Lord Muhammad, and greet them with peace.' At least a third of the manuals which Miss Padwick collected consisted of variations on this single sentence. In praising Muhammad every detail of his figure is treasured and loved, and many names and epithets are lavished upon him in oriental custom. As there are ninety-nine, or more up to a thousand, Most Beautiful Names of God, so there are names of the Prophet which are recited in hymns and litanies. On the human side he is called the man of sound reason, the hero of the sword, the devoted evangelist. As more superhuman he is hailed as the one to whom the stones and trees and birds did homage, at whose light the flowers opened and the fruits

[3] *Muslim Devotions*, 1961, p. 145.

93

matured. He is the hero of the Night Ascent, his legendary flight to Jerusalem and then to the seventh heaven, when he traversed the seven spheres and for him the moon opened out. From God he obtained the devotions for his people, and at the judgement he will be the intercessor for them.

There are special relationships of the Prophet with the whole creation; for the sea and its monsters; for wild and domestic animals; for the prophets and angels; for jinns and devils; in the Law, the Gospel, and all Holy Books. In creation stories the Light of Muhammad was created nine thousand years before the rest of creation, and his name was written on the base of the throne of God. When Adam went out from paradise he saw the name of Muhammad everywhere and he asked 'who is this?' and God replied, 'thy child, but for whom I should not have created thee.'

For the mystic, but also for simple believers, the beloved Prophet is blessed everywhere: 'O Lord, call down a blessing on Muhammad in the cooing of the doves, in the hovering of the birds, in the pasturing of cattle, in the excellence of the strong, in the might of the full-grown.'[4] Muhammad is the pattern for his people, in prayer and in the rest of life. One importance of the pilgrimage, which is a duty to all Muslims at least once in a lifetime, but undertaken by many as often as they can manage it, is the closeness that it brings to the Prophet. Every sacred place in the holy city of Mecca and the sites outside are linked with the mission of Muhammad, and his living presence is felt to reside at his tomb in Medina.

It is sometimes held that Islam is a simple religion, contrasted with the complexity of Christianity, but clearly there is more subtlety and depth than some exponents have indicated, and this helps to explain why any criticism or even slighting comparison of the Prophet is rejected with anger by Muslims, the hurt that is

---

[4] *Muslim Devotions*, pp. 139, 146, 257.

felt for the beloved figure who is believed to be sinless like all prophets, and the greatest of them all.

Response to Muhammad

At a conference held at Tripoli, Libya, in 1975, a Christian participant said that 'there is an issue that disturbs Muslims more than any other in their approach to Christians. It is the silence and reserve of Christians regarding Muhammad ... They do not understand why we refuse to grant Muhammad the respect they themselves grant to the person of Jesus.'[5]

The Muslim attitude to Jesus will be considered in the next chapter, here it may be asked whether all Christians do refuse to respect Muhammad, whether they should, or whether it is not the 'silence and reserve' that is the greatest problem.

In 1984 Dr Kenneth Cragg wrote on *Muhammad and the Christian, A question of Response*. Dr Cragg had written many books on Islam, had travelled and lived in the Middle East for some forty-five years, and was assistant Anglican Bishop of Jerusalem. In this book he shows what an important question the Christian attitude to Muhammad is, and how rarely it has been explored with sympathy on both Christian and Muslim sides. In his bibliography of some of the most important books for a general understanding of Islam, he notes that on Islam and the Prophet in general the list of books is too rich even for partial listing. But, sadly, 'relating to the immediate theme of the title it is almost nil.'

Dr Cragg tackles this important subject with all the care that would be expected of such a careful writer, fully informed of the history, doctrines, and complex relationships of Islam and Christianity. He indicates the problem, of respect for the autonomy of Islam, but also of loyalty to the mind of Christ. He surveys the history of the life of Muhammad, the political

[5] Quoted in *Muhammad and the Christian*, p. ix.

elements in his career and in later Islam, and then gives due attention to the personal devotion to Muhammad in Islam, the Prophet as both example of life and sign of God. At the end he quotes the Koran itself as saying 'let the people of the Gospel decide by what God has sent' (5, 47/51).

In a general way, and from the viewpoint of a Roman Catholic layman, R. C. Zaehner had expressed his feelings some time ago. The claim that Muhammad was a prophet had been a stumbling-block to Christians in the past and many writers of comparative religion still preferred to by-pass it. Yet 'there is no criterion by which the gift of prophecy can be withheld from him unless it is withheld from the Hebrew prophets too', because the Koran reveals such an overwhelming sense of the Divine Being in relation to a people who had not known him. 'That Muhammad was a genuine prophet and that the authentic voice of prophecy made itself heard through him, I for one find it impossible to disbelieve on any rational grounds—assuming, of course, that God exists and makes himself known through prophets.'[6]

Kenneth Cragg is more careful, recognizing the prophetic office of Muhammad but reserving some judgements. 'The Christian conscience must develop a faithful appreciation of the Qur'ān and thereby participate with Muslims in Muhammad within that community of truth as to God and man, creation and nature, law and mercy, which they afford. But such community in truth will never cease to stand in need of those measures of grace and love, of sin and redemption, which are distinctive to the Gospel and which must remain incompatible with the original assumptions of Islamic *Jihād*.'[7]

Some Christians will reject this positive but critical position, and many Muslims may do so, but 'its acknowledgement of Muhammad rests on authentically Christian/Biblical grounds.'

[6] R. C. Zaehner, *At Sundry Times*, 1958, p. 27.
[7] *Muhammad and the Christian*, pp. 141, 159, 152.

And finally, 'if, restoring Jesus' principle, we question or regret the Caesar in Muhammad, it will only be for the sake, in their Quranic form, of those same "things of God", which move us to acknowledge him.'

As for the mystical love of Muhammad, there is 'an interiority in all faiths where the outsider cannot really penetrate.' But there are distinctive devotions, 'the *imitatio Muhammadi* is one, the *imitatio Christi* another.'

Chapter Nine

KORAN AND BIBLE

City of Wrong

IN 1957 the State Prize for Literature was awarded in Cairo to Dr Kamel Hussein, a surgeon and teacher, for his book *City of Wrong*. This work, which aroused great interest in Egypt and has since been translated into several languages including English, is a historical novel about the events of Good Friday.

'City of Wrong', Qaryah Zālimah in Arabic, is a phrase taken from the Koran where it is said that God 'destroyed many a city of wrong', but also that he forbore 'many a city of wrong in its wrong-doing and took hold of it and it returned to God' (Koran 22, 44–47). The cities are not named and they could be Mecca, or Jerusalem, or Rome. In Dr Hussein's book the city is primarily ancient Jerusalem for wronging Jesus, and through him the will of God, on Black Friday.

Bishop Kenneth Cragg, the English translator of this book, explains that the City of Wrong 'symbolizes humanity at large', it is 'representative of the wrongness of the world'. And he continues, 'no reader need suppose that here is some kind of subtle reproach of Jewry, masquerading as a lament over the crucifixion, such as has been known at times in the West'. On the contrary there is a depth of 'Muslim self-criticism', since all mankind is the City of Wrong, sinning against humanity and against God himself.[1]

Kamel Hussein's historical novel is a striking example of an attempt to understand another religion, Christianity, elucidate one of its major themes, and discover universal truths within it, from the different viewpoint of the writer's own religion, Islam. It is not that Muslims have not studied the Bible before. They

[1] *City of Wrong*, English translation, Amsterdam 1959, p. xvi.

98

have done so, both Old and New Testaments, from the very beginning, with the Prophet Muhammad himself, the Koran in its narratives, and countless Muslim scholars and commentators down history. Both Jews and Christians and their holy books, Torah and Evangel, are recognized and honoured in the Koran, the scriptures being true revelations of God. If their followers are faithful to the scriptures it is expressly stated, several times, that Jews, Christians (Nasārā), and 'whoever has believed in God and the Last Day, and has acted uprightly, have their reward 'with their Lord' (2, 59 etc.).

But despite this respect for Jewish and Christian prophets and teachings there remain important doctrinal differences between Christianity and Islam, and one of the most outstanding of these is the problem of the Crucifixion of Jesus. From the earliest days of Islam, in the Koran itself, it seems that the physical reality of the Crucifixion was denied. The crucial Koranic verse reads, 'they did not kill him, and did not crucify him, but he was counterfeited for them. ... They certainly did not kill him. Nay, God raised him to himself' (4, 156).

From a non-Muslim critical viewpont there may seem to be here a reminiscence of those early Christian heretics, the Docetics, who maintained that Jesus only 'seemed' (dokein) to suffer. The apocryphal Acts of John in the second century declared that Jesus appeared to John in a cave during the crucifixion and told him, 'nothing of the things which they will say of me have I suffered. ... I was pierced, yet I was not smitten; hanged, and I was not hanged'. The Koran, however, does not suggest a mere appearance of Jesus floating about above the earth, and elsewhere it insists on his true humanity, asserting that both Jesus and his mother Mary 'ate food' (5, 79).

Nor does the Koran state, as some Gnostics suggested, that a substitute was crucified in the place of Jesus, such as Simon of Cyrene who carried the cross, Judas who hanged himself, or Pilate who condemned Jesus. Whatever may have been suggested in the past, Dr Hussein affirms that 'no cultured Muslim believes in this nowadays'. The Koran is concerned with the power and will of God, and it seems to consider that it would have been impossible to destroy the Messiah of God.

The context of the central verse (4, 156) is the unbelief of Jews, probably those of Medina, who declared that Jesus could not be the Messiah because he had been killed. So the Koran criticizes them 'for violating their covenant, unbelief in the signs of God, killing the prophets without justification'. They had spoken 'against Mary a mighty slander', perhaps accusing her of impurity because she had borne Jesus without a husband. Then they declared, 'we killed the Messiah, Jesus, son of Mary, the messenger of God'. To which it is firmly retorted, 'they did not kill him'.

Despite this apparent firm denial of the crucifixion there are other places in the Koran which do refer to 'the day of the death' of Jesus, and of God bringing his 'term to an end' (19, 34; 3, 48). I have discussed these verses elsewhere, trying to indicate to the more traditional Muslim that there are perhaps two sides to the question in the Koranic verses themselves.[2]

But throughout the Islamic world, from the earliest times and down the ages, the crucifixion of Jesus has been denied. The Koran continued, 'they certainly slew him not, no indeed, God raised him to himself . . . and there is not one of the People of the Book but will surely believe in him before his death, and on the day of resurrection he will be a witness regarding them'. This might suggest some kind of Ascension before the Cross, rather than a Resurrection, and then final belief in Jesus by all the People of the Book, (Jews, Christians and Muslims), and acceptance by him at Resurrection Day.

Christians, apart from a few early Gnostics, and Jews also, have never doubted that the Crucifixion was a fact, however it

---

[2] *Jesus in the Qur'ān*, 1965, and see K. Cragg, *Jesus and the Muslim*, 1985.

may have been interpreted doctrinally. Modern Muslims know about this flat contradiction between the religions. Moreover, they are uneasily aware that secular historians in the West also accept the Crucifixion as a historical fact. If Jesus was a man, who really lived (and very few writers of any merit deny this), then he must have died, sharing the common lot of mankind. There is no serious reason to doubt the basic fact of the Cricifixion. So what does an othodox Muslim think today, in view of the apparent assertion of the Koran that Jesus, alone of all men, did not die? The Koran seems to accept that Jesus had no human father, since it relates the announcement of his virginal birth or conception, attributed to God's powerful word alone, saying 'Be, and it is'. Adam also had no human father, but he died and Jesus did not, on the traditional interpretation.

It is this problem that Kamel Hussein tackled in his imaginative reconstruction, *City of Wrong*. It presents an outline of the events leading up to Good Friday in which the high priests and the disciples, who are not named in the Koran but known through the Bible, and other lay figures all appear to develop the story and draw out its meaning. All the details cannot be given here, but the book may be recommended for devotional as well as textual study, during Lent or before Seder. The book may be difficult to obtain since it has been allowed to go out of print and a kindly publisher might consider a reprint.

Briefly, Dr Hussein's book declares that Jesus was rejected by the City of Wrong, standing for humanity in general. In the introduction Dr Cragg says that the Muslim holy book does not deny the Cross, 'in a very crucial sense it affirms it', for the Cross is the deed of rejection of human teaching and divine love. Dr Hussein, after long dialogues between priests, disciples, and people, concludes that Jesus was taken out to Golgotha. 'It was noon time and the sky was clear. Then thick clouds rolled up from every direction in a few minutes. . . . For three hours the whole land was darkened.' When the darkness lifted Jesus had gone, but 'each of the bystanders had exactly the same set of beliefs. . . . None had changed his convictions', save one who 'returned to his home a believer'.[3] In other words, Jesus was intended for crucifixion, but apparently he was not killed visibly for, as the Koran said, 'God raised him to himself'.

This is as far as a sympathetic, learned but orthodox Muslim could go, in public at least. It is suggested that Jesus was killed in intent, but not in fact, for he was raised to heaven and will come again before the Last Day as Muslims generally have believed.

But this does not fully bridge the gap between Islam and Christianity, · or indeed Judaism. The real crucifixion was stressed by the Apostles' Creed in hammering phrases: 'He suffered under Pontius Pilate, was crucified, dead and buried, he descended into hell'. For the Christian, and doubtless for the Jew as well, crucifixion in intent is worlds apart from death in fact, physical, mortal, final. In long conversations with Kamel Hussein in Cairo I gained the impression that perhaps he did think that Jesus had actually physically died, which could be maintained on other Koranic verses. But he could not say so openly, because Muslim opinion still today would strongly repudiate such a change from traditional orthodox views, and his book would remain unread and perhaps without its State Prize.

The problem of *City of Wrong* is a notable example of some of the difficulties in the encounter of religions. It illustrates some of the problems in understanding another religion, seeing matters from another viewpoint, and particular questions that arise when religions have some common elements, as in Christianity, Islam or Judaism. The special disagreement on the Crucifixion is unusual, though critical, and there are other more general areas of conflicting traditions and interpretations.

[3] *City of Wrong*, pp. 179, 192.

Jesus in the Koran

'We respect Jesus, why do you not respect Muhammad?' ask many Muslims and *City of Wrong* shows how far some modern Muslims are prepared to go in respect for and understanding of Jesus. But from the earliest days, from the Koran itself, Jesus has been revered in the Muslim world. His name is followed by the blessing, 'on whom be peace', on Muslim lips, as their own prophet is similarly blessed. It is claimed that all Muslim devotional books praise Jesus, and while this is a pious exaggeration many of them do take him as an example and more. Sufi mystics praised Jesus for his poverty and purity, and called him 'the seal of the saints'. The biographers of the martyr Hallaj claimed that he identified himself with Jesus in his sufferings and, like him, prayed to God to pardon his executioners.

In the Koran Jesus receives a greater number of honourable titles than any other figure of the past. Moses and Abraham may be mentioned more times, because of the narratives in which they appear, but Jesus is more highly honoured in the Koran and in countless mystical writings later. The Koran calls Jesus a 'sign', a 'mercy', a 'witness' and an 'example'. He is called by his name Jesus under the Arabic form Isa, by the titles Messiah (Christ) and Son of Mary, and by names such as Messenger, Prophet, Servant, Word and Spirit of God. Three chapters of the Koran are named after references to Jesus, and he is mentioned in fifteen chapters and ninety-three verses. He is always spoken of with reverence, without a breath of criticism, for he is held to be a sinless prophet and the Christ.

Mary, the mother of Jesus, is the only woman called by her proper name in the Koran and chapter nineteen is named after her Maryam, giving one of the two accounts of the annunciation and birth of Jesus from Mary. Other women are mentioned in the Koran but they are not named, such as the wives of Noah, Pharaoh and Zachariah, and the Queen of

Sheba. Mary is spoken of as preserved from Satan and defended against attacks of scandal, and like the prophets she came to be regarded as sinless. According to a Koranic story Mary was preserved by Zachariah in the temple and she was fed supernaturally. She gave birth to Jesus away from home, under a tree, and when she was accused by her people of impropriety the child Jesus himself spoke in her defence from the cradle.

Twenty-three times in the Koran Jesus is called Son of Mary, and this title was used of him also in later Islam. This is strange, since Son of Mary appears only once in the Bible, in Mark 6, where the parallel passages in Luke and Matthew change it to Son of Joseph and Son of the Carpenter respectively. But although rare in the Bible and later Christian usage, the title Son of Mary appeared fifteen times in an apocryphal Syriac Infancy Gospel of about the fifth century, followed by an Arabic Infancy Gospel of a century or two later.

The title Son of Mary has been said by one modern Muslim commentator to show that Jesus 'was a mortal like other prophets of God', but Baidawi, a classical exegete of the thirteenth century, remarked that the angels used this title to call attention to the fact that Jesus would be born without a father, since children are usually called after the father. Others have suggested that it would be an insult to call a man after his mother rather than his father, but there are plenty of Arab men who were called after their mothers. Since the Koran always honours Jesus, and relates the Virgin Birth, it would seem that Mary is indicated as his mother because of her prominence and purity.

It might be more strange that this title has been so rare in Christian usage, apart from a few litanies and hymns. Mary was always honoured, but her perpetual virginity came to be an item of popular faith, though without biblical foundation, and she came to be revered for her own sake as God-bearer or Mother of God, or Mother of Christ in the Nestorian interpretation. A female object of devotion became important in both Orthodox and Catholic churches, as it has been in Hinduism and Buddhism, though this element has been strangely lacking in Islam.

The Koran refers to the healing miracles of Jesus, healing the blind, cleansing the lepers, raising the dead. Unfortunately it repeats an apocryphal Christian story of Jesus 'creating figures like birds from clay, and breathing into them so that they became birds', by the permission of God. The infant Jesus speaking in the cradle can also be paralleled from the Arabic Infancy Gospel and may be traced back to the boy Jesus talking to the teachers in the temple.

In chapter five of the Koran, 'The Table', Jesus is said to have asked God to send down a table from heaven, 'to be a festival to us', and parallels have been suggested to both the feeding of the five thousand and the Last Supper, which became the chief Christian 'festival'.

The Koran does not give many direct parallels to the teachings of Jesus, and it may be that the Christians whom Muhammad met were more familiar with a few figures and stories of the Gospels than with the details of teaching. The Gospel is called Injil, Evangel, which was given to Jesus, which was said to confirm the Torah, the Mosaic Law which had gone before, and to provide 'guidance and light'. Apart from the narratives of birth and the Last Supper, the principal sayings common to the Gospel and the Koran are not more than about twenty.[4]

One verse of the Koran, however, contains problems for relations with Christians. 'Jesus, son of Mary, said : O children of Israel, I am God's messenger to you, confirming the Torah which was before me, and announcing the good tidings of the messenger who will come after me, bearing the name Ahmad' (61, 6). Ibn Ishaq, who wrote a classic life of Muhammad about a

---

[4] *Jesus in the Qur'ān*, p. 100ff.

hundred years after his death, said that the Gospel of John had given the words of Jesus that the Comforter and Spirit of Truth would come. He commented that this Comforter 'in Syriac is Muhammad; in Greek he is the paraclete'.[5]

Some western commentators say that the words 'whose name is Ahmad', were interpolated into the Koran to show that Jesus prophesied the coming of Muhammad, but if so why did he not use the word Muhammad? It has been assumed in Islam that Ahmad was one name, or one version of a name, of Muhammad, but this has been disputed. On the other hand what appears to be a proper name Ahmad has been interpreted in an adjectival sense, meaning 'worthy of praise'. This would link up with the promise in the Gospel (John 14) of the Paraclete, or Comforter, the Spirit of Truth who would lead into more truth. But in the Islamic world generally Muhammad has been identified with the Paraclete promised by Jesus.

Similar misunderstandings have arisen over the Koranic interpretation of Christian belief in the Trinity. It declares that it is unbelief to 'say that God is the Messiah, son of Mary', or that 'God is one of three', or that Jesus said 'take me and my mother as two gods apart from God'. And it affirms that 'God is only one God; far from his having a son'. Modern Christian interpreters would agree, for they insist that God is one, as both Muslims and Jews maintain. Heretics, or ignorant believers, may have spoken as if the Trinity was three gods, but orthodox Christianity has always insisted on the unity. So Dr Cragg affirms that 'Muslims who debate tritheism are not discussing Christianity'.

The Koran declares that Jesus was 'a sign to all beings', his family was chosen 'above the worlds', and he came in order that God might 'make him a sign to the people and a mercy from us'. His Gospel gave 'guidance and light, confirming the Torah

5 *The Life of Muhammad*, translated by A. Guillaume, 1955, p. 104.

which was before it, and as guidance and admonition to those who show piety' (5, 50).

Illiterate Prophet?

Thomas Carlyle, despite his championship of Muhammad as a heroic prophet, found the Koran 'a wearisome, confused jumble', and he declared that 'nothing but a sense of duty could carry any European through the Koran'. He read it in an imperfect translation, not in the original Arabic, and he did not seem to realize that the Koran is in verse which is difficult to translate and cannot retain this flavour in another language. Further, the Koran as presented is arranged almost in reverse order to its original utterance. After a short first chapter, which is a ritual prayer, the chapters begin with the longest and gradually get shorter until at the end they are often only of two or three verses. So it may be best to begin at the end and work backwards, as some modern translations do.

Starting at the end, unless one uses a rearranged version, there is a vivid impression of the strong staccato prophecies uttered at Mecca, slowly leading to prosy moral and legal injunctions of the longer chapters which were given for the guidance of the Muslim community in Medina. Even then it is not easy, and the Western reader may be helped by taking a theme and tracing it through with the help of an index or a commentary.

The Koran, even more than some other scriptures, is a ritual book. It is recited in Arabic by all Muslims, from Morocco to Mongolia and from England to South Africa, even if Arabic is not their native language. Strictly speaking it cannot be translated, since it was given as 'an Arabic Koran', and so some versions call themselves interpretations. Some Muslims know the whole Koran by heart, others know only a few verses which are recited in the regular times of daily prayer. Hence the Koran, by language and ritual, is sacrosanct and beyond criticism. The later Traditions may be sifted for 'gold in a heap of chaff', as an

Egyptian scholar told me, but the Koran is regarded as the very
Word of God.

Muslims have believed that Muhammad himself was illiterate
and he did not write the Koran but 'recited' the words that came
to him from heaven. After his death scattered fragments that
had been written down by disciples were said to have been
collected from 'scraps of parchment and leather, tablets of stone,
ribs of palm branches, camels' shoulder-blades and ribs, pieces
of board, and the breasts of men.' The Koran speaks of him as
the *ummi* prophet, (7, 156), a word that has been interpreted as
illiterate, or lacking a scripture, or a 'native' prophet of the
community (*umma*). However some modern Muslim
commentators agree that the Prophet could not read or write
before the revelations came to him, since another verse says
'thou didst not recite before it any book, nor transcribe one with
thy right hand' (29, 47). But it is admitted that there is difference
of opinion as to whether he could read or write after the
revelation. Traditionally the first verses to be revealed (96) state:

> Recite in the name of thy Lord who created,
> created man from clots of blood.
> Recite, for thy Lord is the most generous,
> Who taught by the pen.

The belief that Muhammad did not write the Koran himself
seeks to confirm its status as the very Word of God, recited and
not written. But it was written down by Muhammad's
disciples, although still held to be divinely inspired and
preserved. Some Western scholars, like Richard Bell of
Edinburgh in his translation, hold that the Koran was 'actually
written by Muhammad himself' or by others at his dictation. If
this was so, the Koran is unique among the scriptures of the
world's religions in being written by the founder of the faith.

Early Muslim theologians debated the eternity of the Koran,

as Christian theologians discussed the eternity, the unique and only-begotten nature, of the Son of God. The Muslims sought to affirm that the Koran was the Word of God, yet it was not a second power beside God. They declared that 'the Koran is the speech of God, written in the copies, preserved in the memories, revealed to the Prophet. Our pronouncing, writing and reciting the Koran is created, whereas the Koran itself is uncreated.' The Koran is the eternal speech of God, not different from him 'since God has always been speaking'. So when a Muslim theologian quoted the Koran he clinched any argument by saying bluntly, 'God said', and giving chapter and verse.

Fundamentalist Christians refer to the Bible as the Word of God, but the Gospel speaks of Christ as the 'Word made flesh'. So it has been said that the difference from Islam is that it holds to the 'Word made book'.

To the Muslim Muhammad is sinless, the last and greatest prophet, second only to God. The Koran is the very Word of God. But can either be recognized by non-Muslims as giving the truth and worthy of reverence? An eminent British scholar, W. M. Watt, who has written standard works on Muhammad at Mecca and Medina, confesses as an 'amateur' Christian theologian, that 'I hold the Qur'ān to be in some sense the product of a divine initiative and therefore revelation.'[6]

That is a guarded statement and more pointedly an eminent Canadian, W. C. Smith, asks 'Is the Qur'ān the Word of God?' This question, he says, would of course have always been answered with an emphatic affirmative as an article of faith by Muslims. But the question would have been almost as strongly denied by Christians in the past, who regarded the Koran as erroneous, heretical, if not inspired by the devil. Even today the question of the religious truth in the Koran is either repudiated or, worse, ignored.[7] As Kenneth Cragg discovered when

[6] *Islamic Revelation in the Modern World*, 1969, p. 8.
[7] *Questions of Religious Truth*, 1967.

looking for books on the Christian response to Muhammad, on 'the immediate theme of the title it is almost nil'. Yet the question will not go away, in our multi-religious world where religious mingling and challenges are greater than ever before. One beginning of an answer may be that the Koran or part of it can only become the Word of God to us if God speaks to us through it.

Chapter Ten

WHO KILLED CHRIST?

Canadian Views
Some years ago I was asked to take part in a Canadian television programme with the title 'Who Killed Christ?' This tried to include different views of the Crucifixion and responsibility for it, Christian, Jewish, and even Muslim, with discussions with leading figures and lay people in the religions and shots taken in Israel and neighbouring countries.

Having written on Jesus in the Koran, and discussed Muslim difficulties over the question of the historicity or not of the Crucifixion, my part was to indicate that beyond Christian and Jewish debates there were other views worth mentioning. A hall outside Oxford was hired for the programme and against this impressive background, with a copy of the Koran in hand, my role was to sketch briefly the Muslim ideas that Christ had not been killed, and the conclusion for them that the Jews could not be held responsible for the Crucifixion. This could provide a new twist to the old Jewish-Christian debate, though one that perhaps was not so serious nowadays when western-educated Muslims themselves gave different interpretations of the events, as indicated in the last chapter in Kamel Hussein's historical novel.

Looking over the script of the rest of the programme which outlined Christian and Jewish opinions, it was surprising to find a general assumption by the writers that Christians believe that Jesus was killed by the Jews, as a people and including modern Jews who were still held responsible for the death of the one who is claimed as their Messiah. It is common knowledge that some Christians held such views in the past and it was affirmed that some still do in Canada, and no doubt elsewhere. But this could hardly be the general opinion, because it is not current among modern, British, Protestant Christians, at least.

It is perhaps important to affirm that in a lifetime of listening to Christian sermons and teachings, never once have I heard said that the Jews were responsible for the Crucifixion. A brief survey of local church congregations confirmed this impression. When asked, 'who killed Jesus?' the commonest answer, after some reflection on this unusual question, was, 'the Creed says Pontius Pilate'. Others replied, it was the Romans, or local officials of the first century, or the priests, or a mob artificially stimulated to demand his execution, though Roman soldiers carried it out. Nobody suggested that the Jewish people, as a whole in the past, and certainly not later or today, were responsible for the Crucifixion. Some Irish Roman Catholics who were questioned asserted that their priests had never made this charge, though one admitted that ignorant lay people had occasionally said so.

It may be asked, were these people who were interrogated not aware of the verse in Matthew's Gospel (27, 25): 'His blood be on us, and on our children'? It must be admitted that some were not aware of this verse, or had not thought about it, because not all Christians are well read in the Bible or theologically trained. Those who knew the verse commented that it only referred to that generation or the next, it was a mob's acceptance of responsibility, if Matthew had not invented it, since this statement is not found in the other Gospels. The better informed quoted another verse earlier in Matthew (23, 36): 'all these things shall come upon this generation', which was paralleled in Luke, but they noted that it referred to the destruction of Jerusalem by the Romans in A.D. 70, which was that generation. Matthew was seen as the most Jewish Gospel, and yet the most anti-Jewish, turning against its own people for their unbelief in the Christian cause. Mark is the oldest Gospel, and the general consensus of the four Gospels should be sought in delicate matters of this kind.

Perhaps it should be repeated that no one, in these modern Christian circles, attributed any blame to the Jewish people as such, in the past or as a whole. Yet the assumption of the scripts seemed to be that this is what we think, almost a myth, that Christians believe the Jews killed Christ, and the film tried to set matters right.

Jews and Society

In discussing the religions of the world it is easy to concentrate upon the largest, which after Christianity are the big three: Islam, Hinduism and Buddhism. But Judaism has a special and intimate relation to Christianity, and it is not only a phenomenon of past history but a present community. Many religious societies from Asia, Muslim, Hindu, Sikh, Buddhist, even Parsi, are now to be found in the West, in Dispersions which may affect the interpretation of their faiths in modern times. But the Jews are the oldest non-Christian religious minority here, and although their numbers are exceeded by Muslims in Europe, they are integrated into social life, though religious exchanges have been limited.

The relationships of Jews and Christians have long been difficult, to put it mildly. In the first century Christians were a minority, struggling to establish their own identity. Jesus was a Jew, though Christians often forget this or its implications. All the Christian scriptures, the New Testament, were written by Jews with the possible exception of Luke. Yet although Jesus taught in Aramaic, all the New Testament was written in Greek, testifying to the spread of the faith outside Palestinian Judaism, and the need to put its documents in the international language, as in modern times English might be used.

For the first three centuries Christians were persecuted, at the beginning by Jewish authorities, but rapidly by the Romans who objected both to their inter-racial character and to their refusal to observe the official religion. Many Christians were martyred, from the deaths of Peter and Paul, until the Edict of Toleration signed by the emperors Galerius and Constantine in 311. Christians were then allowed freedom and their own churches, and in 380 Theodosius established the Catholic Christians and threatened secular and sacred punishment to heretics.

The Jews lived as minorities under Romans and Christians, enduring both toleration and hostility. There were pressures towards conversion, though a few voices, such as that of Bernard of Clairvaux, objected to persecution. In the Crusades, ostensibly initiated to free the holy places from the rule of Muslim 'infidels', popular fury was often whipped up against the Jews in western Europe. The Spanish Inquisition persecuted the Jews to a hitherto unsurpassed intensity, partly linked to the efforts to free Spain from Muslim occupation, and seize the goods of both Muslims and Jews.

Secular authorities in the Middle Ages had ambiguous attitudes towards Jews, on the one hand tolerating them as moneylenders and trying to control popular rioting, and on the other hand squeezing them financially dry and then expelling them from cities and countries. A charter of Richard I of England in 1190 granted rights to 'Ysaac, son of Rabbi Joce, and to his children and to their men', but seems to envisage all Jews. It confirmed previous permission to reside in the land freely and honourably, and ordered proper trials in disputes between Christians and Jews.

Richard's charter was an attempt to counter or check popular anti-Jewish riots, since it was signed only six days after a mass suicide of Jews in York. The king's resolve to join the Crusades fanned anti-Jewish fervour, and when they were attacked by a mob in York the Jews barricaded themselves in Clifford's Tower and set fire to it, perishing like the zealots of Masada in A.D. 74.

In 1255 the Jews of Lincoln were supposed to have captured a young Christian boy called Hugh, and to have tortured and crucified him in mockery of the Crucifixion of Christ. This is an example of the 'blood-libel' which was common in the Middle Ages in which Jews were said to steal unbaptized babies and eat them, thus explaining the high infant mortality of those days. When the Jews had been 'liquidated', other scapegoats for the ills of society had to be found, such as the so-called 'witches' who were said to meet in 'synagogues' and on 'sabbaths', and to engage in child cannibalism.

A late version of the Ballad of Hugh of Lincoln simply says that he was 'stickit like a swine' for breaking a Jew's window with a football, but clearly there were much deeper motives suspected in the accusations. Sadly Chaucer in the Prioresses Tale about 1380 mentions young Hugh of Lincoln 'slayn also with cursed Jewes'. He more fully slanders the Jews 'in Asie, in a greet citie', for 'foule usure and lucre of vilanye', going on to the murder of a child of 'Cristen blood'.

In 1290 Edward I, conqueror of Wales and Hammer of the Scots, expelled the 16,000 Jews of England for extortionate usury. He had earlier hanged 280 of them for supposed forgery and money-clipping. Edward had joined the last Crusade and wanted to lead another, and was supported by popular fanaticism. Not till the time of Oliver Cromwell were Jews permitted to return to England, in 1656, both for their financial and religious interests.

The attitude of the church was at times less favourable to the Jews than that of the state, especially among the preaching friars who stirred up the masses at Easter and in support of the Crusades, although there were more tolerant attitudes at times among the higher clergy. But the Fourth Lateran Council of 1215 condemned the Jews for usury in the 'perfidy' of 'exacting interest', decreed that Jews and Saracens should be distinguished from Christians in dress, should not appear in public in Lent, should not be appointed to public office, should not observe Jewish rites if they had taken Christian baptism, and ordered that interest should not be paid on Jewish debts while their debtors were absent on Crusades.

Jews in Europe were not only different by religion, but they came to be kept in ghettos, an Italian word possibly from *borghetto*, a small borough, to which Jews were confined by a papal bull in 1595. These restrictions were largely swept away by the French revolution and the Enlightenment of the eighteenth century, and the emancipation of Jews followed in western Europe.

Persecutions in eastern Europe from the end of the nineteenth century led to large emigrations to Britain, France and America. The rise of the Zionist movement and return to the land of Israel was small at first, but it was greatly accelerated by Jews looking for refuge from central and eastern Europe. In the twentieth century came the worst horror of all time, when nearly six million Jews were murdered in the Holocaust of Nazi concentration camps.

Jesus the Jew
The continual persecutions of Jews by Christians, for at least a thousand years, which was partly responsible for Nazi attitudes towards them, effectively prevented any religious dialogue between Jews and Christians. Persecutors and persecuted must have felt that they had nothing to learn from each other, but scorn and fear. On the one hand the Jews believed themselves to be the chosen people, though strangely suffering, and rejected the claim that Jesus was the Messiah, and they continue to this day to 'believe with perfect faith in the coming of the Messiah and, though he tarry, I will wait daily for his coming'.

On the other hand Christians, even when kindly disposed, could only pray for the conversion of Jews. Until recently the regular Anglican collect for Good Friday prayed: 'Have mercy upon all Jews, Turks, Infidels, and Hereticks, and take from them all ignorance, hardness of heart, and contempt of thy Word.' While the Roman Catholic church described the Crucifixion as 'deicide', a theologically questionable term, and only at the Second Vatican Council in 1965 was this 'deicide' no longer blamed on the Jews, and it was agreed that they were not 'rejected by God and accursed'.

In such conditions, to ask 'Who killed Christ?', assumed that Jesus was the Christ, which Jews had constantly denied, and on their side even Jesus the Jew had little attraction. With all the attacks upon Jews, often with lynching or torture, even recognition of the virtues and teaching of the human Jesus was very rare among Jews. But in more liberal modern times, and since the rise of critical study of the Bible, Jewish scholars have turned to the study of his life and have contributed to both academic and religious communication.

Dr Joseph Klausner, a Jewish scholar born in Russia, published in 1922, in Hebrew, a study of the life and teaching of Jesus, entitled *Jesus of Nazareth*. He remarked that hitherto there had never been any book on Jesus in Hebrew which had not had either a Christian propagandist aim of bringing Jews to Christianity, or a Jewish religious aim of rendering Christianity obnoxious to Jews. His long study need not be discussed in detail here, but it may be noted that he regarded the main strength of Jesus to lie in his ethical teaching. If we 'preserved only the moral precepts and parables, the Gospels would count as one of the most wonderful collections of ethical teaching in the world'.

More recently Dr Geza Vermes of Oxford published a small but detailed booklet in 1981 on *The Gospel of Jesus the Jew*. He is a member of the synagogue with which I have the closest connection and his work is sympathetic and scholarly, short but of great importance.

Dr Vermes makes a number of points as a historian reading the Gospels. The first is a surprising criticism of the negative and pessimistic attitudes of modern critical Christian scholars towards the Gospel records. The famous form-critic Rudolf Bultmann had declared that 'we can now know almost nothing concerning the life and personality of Jesus, since the early Christian sources show no interest in either.' The Gospels, he thought, do not represent the thoughts and aims of Jesus, but doctrines to meet the needs of the early church.

But Dr Vermes affirms that the theological convictions of the evangelists were no more incompatible with a concern for history than is a political or philosophical conviction. Why did the evangelists choose *biography* if they were preoccupied with teaching Christian doctrine? There was no Jewish convention that the sayings of the sages should be recorded in this way, and there is no similar biography in rabbinic literature or the Dead Sea Scrolls. Indeed the evangelists inserted sayings of Jesus which seemed to conflict with some of the teachings of the early church, such as unwillingness to announce himself as the Messiah. Further, some elements in the story of Jesus are confirmed in several ways; his kindness to the outcasts of society is shown by events, stories, sayings and parables.

Jesus was called 'a prophet mighty in deed and word' in the Gospels, and the Jewish historian Josephus wrote of him as a 'wise man' famous for his 'marvellous deeds'. So Dr Vermes says that Jesus the teacher cannot be properly understood without seeing him also as a man of God, the holy man of Galilee, the *hasid*, 'pious one'. Compared with other hasids 'no objective and enlightened student of the Gospels can help but be struck by the incomparable superiority of Jesus'.[1]

Dr Vermes says much more: Jesus was a healer as well as a teacher, in the succession of charismatic prophets like Elijah and Elisha, healing body and mind, fighting evil now because his word heralded the coming of the kingdom. He regarded God

[1] *The Gospel of Jesus the Jew*, pp. 10, 18.

particularly as Father, his favourite term, preserved in the Aramaic even in the Greek Gospels, not just as a childish name since it is used also in solemn situations, but showing a relation to the Father and his kingdom. His piety went deeper than religiosity, not merely accepting but positively seeking out the outcasts, and honoured by the sarcastic nickname, 'friend of tax-collectors and sinners'. There is a universalism in his commandment to love one's enemies and imitate the Father of all who cares for all. Perhaps enough has been said here to indicate what may be learnt from a Jewish scholar when religious dialogue is at last possible.

In a comparable manner Professor David Daube discussed some crucial Christian teachings from a Jewish point of view in his lecture *He that Cometh* in 1966. Looking at the Jewish Passover eve service, and the Christian Last Supper, he fastens on the *Aphiqoman*. This is a fragment of the unleavened bread which is set aside at the beginning of the meal, and may be hidden to give children a chance to look for it. This word is neither Hebrew nor Aramaic, but is Greek though its meaning has long been debated. It may mean 'the Coming One', 'He that Cometh', and would symbolize the Hidden Messiah.

The Last Supper, says Professor Daube, presupposes a ritual like that of 'the Coming One'. The idea was applied to the situation when Jesus, at the end of the meal, broke off a fragment of unleavened bread as the Messiah. He said '*this* is my body', referring to the ritual of 'the Coming One', and revealing at last that he was the Messiah, now being made known.

Even the Lord's Prayer, so constantly recited, contains the hope of the hidden but Coming One, says Professor Daube. It prays 'thy kingdom come', and 'lead us not into temptation, but deliver us from evil', that is from the tribulations before the Messianic Age. But at its heart it has a curious word usually translated 'daily' bread. In Greek this is *epiousios*, but apart from the parallel passages in Matthew and Luke the word occurs nowhere else in the New Testament or Greek literature. So what does it mean? It is often translated as the bread 'for the coming day', but this could be the bread 'of the Coming One'. And in Rabbinic literature there are familiar concepts of 'the bread of the World that cometh' or 'the bread of the kingdom', as Jews still pray for the final redemption 'speedily, in our days'. The Lord's Prayer contains this hope for the coming Kingdom and Messiah, hidden at first, made known in the Last Supper.

The Didache, a Christian 'teaching' of the late first or early second century, speaks of the Lord's Supper as 'the broken bread scattered on the mountains', and ends the meal with 'Maranatha, Our Lord cometh'. And much earlier Paul had said, 'the bread which we break, is it not the communion of the body of Christ? For we being many are one bread, one body.' So again light comes from Jewish tradition, illuminating early Christian teaching and later practice. The benefit is both in Jewish study of Christian documents, and in Christian learning from Rabbinic teachings and customs.

Dialogue and Ritual
Being invited to become president of the London Society of Jews and Christians was an honour and a way into closer relations between Jews and Christians in the city, after many studies and discussions with members of African and farther Asian religions.

This society organizes regular discussions and debates between Jews and Christians, orthodox and liberal. It has an annual garden party in the grounds of Westminster Abbey, by kind permission of the Dean, and a lecture at Church House. But it seeks to bring understanding of Judaism and Christianity as practised religions as well as doctrinal systems. There have been joint celebrations of Christmas and Hanukkah. Jews believe that Jesus existed, he was born, and his birthday may be honoured, though Christians are not inhibited from giving their own interpretations of the feast. Hanukkah also comes in December, commemorates the 'dedication' of the temple after the Maccabees had defeated the Syrians who defiled it, in 165 B.C., and is signalled by the kindling of lights, one each day, on an eight-branched candlestick. As historical religions, Judaism and Christianity need to understand each other's traditions.

Songs, stories and appropriate food can also be shared at Passover with Easter. But every other year there is a Model Seder at the synagogue to which Christians and other friends are invited. The Seder is the 'order' of the service which is held in Jewish homes at the beginning of Passover, and its ritual is in the Haggadah, 'narration'.

The Seder is a festival and on a large table in front of the head of the family, or whoever conducts the service, are the following elements: three wafers of matzot, unleavened bread; roasted lamb bone and egg; a dish of grated horseradish or sliced lettuce; a dish of parsley or cress; a dish of salt water; a dish of charoset, apples, almonds, raisins, cinnamon, with a little wine; and two unlighted candles. In front of every participant is a wine glass, with a large goblet in front of the celebrant, which is called Elijah's Cup. This indicates the belief in the coming of Elijah as the forerunner of the Messiah, but it also indicates that any stranger, Jew or Gentile, who might come in is welcome, expressing the spirit of hospitality and brotherhood.

The Seder proceeds with prayers and indications of the symbolism of the various elements at different points. The service recalls the redemption of the Hebrew people from Egypt at the Exodus, and many other deliverances. The youngest member of the family asks why this night is different from all others, and is told of the history of his people. Joining in prayers, readings, psalms and thanksgiving, the family and people praise God that despite countless sufferings his presence has been with them. Had God only brought the people out of Egypt, or only fed them in the desert, or only given the Sabbath, or only given the Law, or only brought them into the land of Israel, or only built the Temple, or only sent the prophets, each would have been enough. But God has done all these things.

The law is read, the Shema, 'hear' O Israel, and the significance of the symbols explained with the offering of the lambs at Passover, the unleavened bread at the hasty flight, the bitter herbs in Egypt, and other elements related to feasts and festivals. At the end children look for the Aphiqoman and the meal ends with blessings, psalms, popular songs, eating and drinking.

To the non-Jew the Seder is impressive for its narration of history and expression of history in the symbols. Both Judaism and Christianity claim to be historical religions, but Judaism has an attachment to land and place that an international religion tends to overlook. The communal spirit, with the participation of the family, from the youngest member, and the open door to strangers, is an expression of that hospitality which is so traditional a virtue in oriental countries and which Judaism has retained despite centuries of persecution. That this religion has been maintained, with faith in the mysterious providence of God despite agelong suffering which culminated in the unspeakable horrors of the Holocaust, is a marvel to which faithful Jews bear witness.

Some Christian churches in recent years have organized a Christian Passover service, which uses the symbolism and procedure of the Seder, but culminates in the Lord's Supper. To Jews this would generally be an unacceptable deviation, but it recalls the fact that Jesus celebrated the first Passover Seder meal at the Last Supper, that he was a Jew, and that Jewish history is inextricably entwined with Christian. Belief in Jesus as the Messiah remains the fundamental difference between Christians and Jews, beyond differences of language and ritual, and each has to learn to respect the convictions of the other.

That Christians can learn from Judaism, and show repentance

for the intolerance and ill-treatment of the past, does not imply approval of all the actions of the State of Israel. It is difficult, but not impossible, to sympathize with the aspirations of both Jews and Arabs. Some of the most severe criticisms of belligerent actions by Israel come from Jews. When Lebanon was invaded in 1982 a London liberal Jewish minister, Rabbi John Rayner, declared that 'there is surely not even a remote possibility of morally justifying the ferocity of the bombardment of west Beirut.' Judaism had been one of the great moral teachers of mankind, but the writer Chaim Bermant wrote that the name of Israel was 'now a source of reproach'. The moral sensitivity of Judaism remained and was a challenge to Christians. Lebanese Maronite Christian militia massacred hundreds of Muslim men, women and children in refugee camps, but the Israeli authorities were in charge. The Chief Rabbi of the United Hebrew Congregations of the British Commonwealth, Sir Immanuel Jakobovits, now said that 'no condemnation can be strong enough of those who perpetrated or connived in this outrage'. Jews and Christians remain under the judgement and the mercy of God, and are commanded to 'let justice roll down as waters, and righteousness as a mighty stream'.

To Christians Judaism is our mother, or perhaps it may be said that to Protestants our own church of England or another is our mother, the Roman Catholic church is our grandmother and Judaism our great-grandmother. There are close family ties and a common spiritual heritage. Judaism, Christianity and Islam are called the Semitic religions, by descent from the mythical Shem, but more significant religiously is descent from Abraham or Moses.

The Koran claims a spiritual descent for all of us from Abraham, as well as a physical descent for the Arabs from Ishmael. 'Abraham was not a Jew, nor was he a Christian, but he was a God-fearer, a Muslim [a surrendered man], not one of the polytheists' (Koran 3, 60). If the Jews were named after Judah, then this Koranic statement is strictly correct, since Abraham was Judah's great-grandfather. But the meaning is deeper, that Abraham was the progenitor of all true believers in one God. It recalls Paul's argument that those who have faith like Abraham are his children (Galatians 3, 7).

There is a common ancestry and faith in this religious succession, an overriding monotheism, a belief in one God in our three religions. And the vulgar objection that we worship God whereas the Muslims worship Allah and the Jews worship Jehovah (whose name is too sacred for them to mention), has little more sense than to claim that the English worship God while the French adore Dieu, the Germans Gott and the Spaniards Dios. There are many names, and many and imperfect understandings of him, but there is one God, who is over all, blessed for ever.

Bishop Kenneth Cragg, in his book *The Call of the Minaret* and other writings has tried to clear away misunderstandings of Christian doctrine and present the faith in ways that Muslims could appreciate, and to some degree this could be said to Jews also. First, he affirms that the Trinity 'does not consist, as there has been a tendency . . . to suppose, of God, Jesus and the Virgin Mary'. Then, 'there is absolutely no reason to insist' that the term 'Father' necessarily implies paternity in the physical sense. 'It goes without saying that God does not have children as his creatures do.' So 'the terms "Father" and "Son" have no physical significance and are used analogically'. The classic Christian expression of the divine activity is that 'God was in Christ', rather than that 'Jesus was God'. So for all of these three religions 'we cannot proceed except on the understanding that we are . . . firmly and equally believers that God is One'. We stand 'squarely in the Hebrew tradition: "The Lord our Lord is ONE Lord." '[2]

---

[2] *The Call of the Minaret*, 1956, pp. 308, 315f.

Chapter Eleven

AFRICAN AFFIRMATION

Scripture of Art

In the nineteen fifties a museum in Leyden sent to the University College of Ibadan, Nigeria, some photographs of a statue they had bought. It looked old and crude and they thought it might be African. But there was an inscription on the chest of the human figure, in characters that resembled ancient Greek. If this was indeed African, from the tropics, then it was very rare and perhaps unique in presenting an ancient example of writing from Africa south of the Sahara desert.

Experts in African art, together with students of religion and history, considered the statue and compared it with other figures, deciding that the style was not African, and soon the truth appeared from Europe that it was one of the 'Moabite fakes'. In 1868 French and German scholars discovered the Moabite Stone which related how Mesha king of Moab had revolted against Omri king of Israel, an event referred to also in the Bible. Following this discovery several hundred pottery figures appeared on international markets and were claimed as Moabite. Some Germans thought them genuine, but the French saw they were fakes, and as their country had just been defeated by Germany in 1870 they were glad to be proved right. They had been made by potters in modern Jerusalem and disappeared from the market for eighty years and now were claimed as African, with inscriptions.

The occasion illustrated the difficulties of studying African religion, which was apparently crude and had no scriptures. I lived nearly twenty years in Africa, mostly teaching in French and English, and can claim among former students in Africa and England not only eminent teachers and clergy, but one of

Africa's leading novelists and a Nobel Peace Prize-winner. But African religion, and African Islam and Christianity, were ideal subjects for study and college vacations provided many opportunities for research.

Yet there were great difficulties in the study, being a foreigner and a white man, working generally through interpreters (or interrupters), and faced with the lack of scriptures to reveal something of the religion in history and from the inside. Tropical Africa had been isolated from the Mediterranean world by arid desert, impenetrable forest and sea. When eventually, only in recent centuries, trade from the outside world did appear in the African tropics, with religious and other cultural influences, it was by Islamic traders using coastal routes, and European traders coming by sea, both avoiding desert and forest.

The art of writing had not appeared in these tropical regions till modern times, for it is a rare invention. Most forms of writing come from either the alphabetic scripts of the Near East or the syllabic characters of China. The peoples of northern Europe were virtually illiterate till writing was brought to them by Christian missionaries, as the Japanese received writing through Buddhist missionaries. The ancient American cultures had temples, pyramids and palaces, but no writing properly so called. So African ignorance of writing came not from inability to express thoughts but isolation from inventions made elsewhere.

The absence of literature from inside the religion meant that it was not possible to discover from scriptures the beliefs and experiences of religious men and women in traditional Africa. In modern times many studies of African religion have been made, but from the outside by foreign investigators, or by educated Africans who no longer hold to the religion of their fathers which they are describing. To some extent this has happened in research in other areas, and there are many studies of Islam, Hinduism and Buddhism by scholars who do not share the religion they describe. But there have also been books by believers, and there are many scriptures of the past which enunciate the basic beliefs and attitudes.

Yet there were means of expression used by Africans, scriptures of a sort, in the arts which Africans developed and whose originality and power have been recognized by European artists such as Picasso, Epstein and Henry Moore. Painting and sculpture, in stone, ivory, brass, wood, clay, cloth and other materials have been used since time immemorial for daily purposes and for important representations. These express people's beliefs from the inside, though their interpretation by others is not always easy, and students of religion have tended to regard art as a separate department instead of an essential tool for religious understanding.

Some of the most ancient forms of African art are paintings and engravings on rocks and walls of caves, and they are found all over Africa, from the Sahara to South Africa. The Bushmen of southern Africa, the oldest inhabitants of the region, painted hunting scenes, with men, women and animals, which seem to have had magico-religious purposes in encouraging the fertility of animals and the skill of hunters. In this they resemble the cave paintings of southern France and northern Spain which date from about 13,000 B.C. Unfortunately the modern Bushmen in Africa no longer practise painting and the interpretation of their art cannot be given in detail.

At Nok in Nigeria there are terracotta heads from about two thousand years ago, and in later centuries at Ife and Esie and other places there are so many stone, bronze and clay figures that they are in veritable treasure-houses. Many of the casts or sculptures of heads are naturalistic, so that when first seen by Europeans they were compared with Greek sculpture or it was suggested that they must have been made by early explorers. But now it is recognized that the style, tradition and subject matter of the sculptures is truly African. Many heads represented kings with crowns or bead veils, which indicated their sacredness. Some are semi-divine figures, founders of dynasties, gods of earth and sea, whose sculptures illustrate themes in mythology.

Life-affirmation

From art as well as modern religion it soon appears that a fundamental characteristic of African belief is in the importance of life on earth. Contrary to the world-denial and asceticism of some Asian and European religions, this world and all its elements are cherished. This appears in beliefs in reincarnation, which in African expressions is rebirth on to this warm earth to perpetuate the family of the past, whereas in Asia it is often an effort to get away from the sufferings of this life into the indescribable bliss of Nirvana. A symbol of rebirth in African art is the snake, which sheds its skin to go on living, and which with its tail in its mouth is an apt representation of an endless circle, a ring of eternity.

The panorama of life is well illustrated in the *mbari*, 'decorated', houses which Igbo people of Nigeria have traditionally erected at special times. These were temporary temples, built at the specific command of a god, but never repaired after construction and soon falling into disrepair. The central figure of such temples is Ala, the great Mother Goddess, the spirit of fertility, and guardian of the dead which as they are buried in the earth are said to be in her pocket. Some of the statues of Ala with a child in her arms have been compared to Italian Madonnas or the Egyptian Isis with her son Horus. The *mbari* buildings have high decorated walls and a central shrine, surrounded by a veranda in which are clay and painted images of human beings and animals of all kinds: chiefs, policemen, traders, women, travellers in sun helmets or on motor cycles, tailors with sewing machines, students with wristwatches, dancing girls, elephants, monkeys, and nurses with patients on stretchers. All life is there, painted with energy and vivid colours, but in the centre sits Ala, mother earth.

In other parts of Africa there are similar mud sculptures and since they are fragile and cannot be exported they are not commercial productions for the tourist market. Some are traditional figures, of gods or their attendants, but new figures are easily taken in and political and Christian statues are mingled with the old.

Often the chief deity is not represented in human form in his temple, such as the well known temple of the storm at Ibadan. Here there is a finely carved screen with wooden images of animals, women, a soldier on a horse and a Muslim with beads, but the storm god is simply indicated by 'thunder stones' in a bowl on the altar.

The supreme creator God, who appears in salutations and stories in most parts of Africa, is never represented by an image, and he usually has neither temple nor special worship. But God is not impotent or absent, he is rather the supreme power that works through lesser beings, and the final court of appeal to whom poor and rich alike may appeal.

Belief in a supreme God was present in most parts of Africa before the missionaries arrived, and belief in life after death was also an ancient and fundamental conviction. Some of the best known African carvings are wooden masks, many of which have been collected by visitors and dispersed to museums throughout the world. The masks are fixed to robes of grass or cloth which are worn by men representing the spirits of the dead, and it is taboo to speak of them as human beings. Some masks are naturalistic, but many are abstract or terrifying, and they indicate the awesomeness and enhanced powers of the spirits. Whatever their form the masks express the universal conviction that death is not the end of life, and also the unity of the living and the dead. The life-affirmation is expressed even in

129

death, so to speak, for the departed go on living and are concerned with the lives and property of their descendants.

Sacred or Profane?

One of the most debated questions in religious studies in general is the distinction between sacred and profane, religious and secular, Christian and agnostic or atheist. On the one hand are those who maintain that religion is essentially an individual concern, dependent on a view of the supernatural that is out of date, and constantly diminishing in specifically religious materials. On the other hand it is declared that the distinction is false, all life is one, God is present everywhere, and even when organizations such as churches become less effective their influence is replaced by other world views, of science or communism, both of which have religious overtones and inspiration.

African art expresses religious attitudes, though they are not always easy to interpret. But all of life is there, gods and animals, ancient chiefs and modern motorcyclists. There is easy adaptation of new materials, musical instruments, printed clothing, concrete in place of clay. But can African art be transferred from one religious faith to another without loss of the primary inspiration? Since Christianity, and Islam, have made great progress in Africa can they adapt African art to their own purposes?

For a long time missionaries and their converts in Africa imported religious pictures and symbols, and regarded the indigenous artefacts as 'heathen', 'pagan', 'idolatrous', if not 'diabolical'. This was expressed with special force against the countless images of women with bare breasts and numerous phallic stones or images. But since the nineteen forties Roman Catholic missionaries, in particular, in West Africa have employed African carvers to illustrate Christian themes, even when they were not Christian converts.

Fr. Kevin Carroll has justified the use of the African carver by saying that 'he is inspired by a humanist rather than a religious spirit'. He rejects the claim that the African artist must be inspired by the exalted religious function of his work, and that he is inspired by a religious vision and sets about his work with devotion. He concludes that the art of the African carver, 'at least that with which I am familiar, is a humanistic rather than a deeply religious art, even when directly concerned with the creation of religious objects'.[1]

Kevin Carroll is a Roman Catholic priest and it is strange to find an agnostic anthropologist and art critic, Ulli Beier, attacking the view that African art is humanistic and declaring that 'of course it is correct to say that a great deal of carving serves no immediate religious function. ... But we must remember that in Yoruba life it is impossible to divide the sacred from the profane'.

Carvers in Christian workshops have produced religious statues, of Christ and the Virgin Mary, and numerous panels with illustrations of events in the life of Jesus and the way of the Cross. Kevin Carroll claims that 'even a pagan carver can soon learn to know and reverence Christ and the saints and can vividly carve the stories and anecdotes concerning them'. Ulli Beier takes up the attack by stating that 'the African carver when he works for the christian workshop abandons the "deeply expressive art" of his religion and settles down comfortably to tell *anecdotes* about Christ'. He goes on to say that 'the Church has been able to provide the carver with new work but not with new inspiration. ... Their figures are dull and puppet-like. ... It is only the christian carvings that give a profane impression'.[2]

Between these two the anthropologist William Fagg suggests a middle way of noting that 'many affinities can be found

[1] *Yoruba Religious Carving*, 1967, pp. 39, 53.
[2] *ibid.*, p. 70.

between Christianity and the "pagan" religions and none is more striking to my mind than the similarity between their fundamental philosophical concepts of "force" and the Christian concept of grace', and he believes that 'Father Carroll has demonstrated the viability of a Christianized traditional art'.[3]

Conditions are changing rapidly in Africa and if the new generations are largely Christian it may be expected that their artists will have Christian inspiration, if they are not deflected into mass productions for the commercial market. A striking contrast between the old and the new may be seen in the two facing chapels in Ibadan university. The great wooden door of the Roman Catholic chapel, a rectangular concrete building designed by Maxwell Fry, has ten small panels of carvings representing scenes from the nativity, crucifixion and resurrection of Jesus, in traditional African style. The Protestant chapel, a great concrete parabola designed by George Pace, has a life size wooden statue of the risen Christ with Mary Magdalene kneeling in front of him. It is more European in style but the carver was an Igbo, Ben Enwonwu, and the faces of his figures are African, showing a combination of cultures.

Lamidi, the carver of the Roman Catholic panels, and of many other churches, is a Yoruba whose father was a 'pagan', his brother is Christian, and he himself is a Muslim. Anywhere else it might be almost unbelievable that a Muslim should carve statues or decorate Christian churches. Lamidi is a practising Muslim, who does not take part in 'pagan' rites, but he claims rightly that the Koran treats Jesus and Mary with great reverence, and that it has much in common with the Bible. African society, contrasted with much of European, is generally tolerant of religious diversity and in the same family there are often followers of different religions, who may observe each

[3] *ibid.*, p. x.

other's festivals where these do not conflict with their own doctrines.

Magic and Mystic

A woman came to a priest for help after a series of misfortunes. After long conversation he dressed in robes, with braided hair, charms in his necklace and bracelets, and his skin covered with white powder. The woman knelt in front of him, while he uttered incantations and dusted her body with the powder. She had brought a fowl and her brow, chest, knees and feet were brushed with its feathers. Then she took a goat that she had also brought by the horns, and following the priest's instructions she placed her forehead three times against that of the goat. She was given a pot of leaves and water to wash her head, and she took a small bamboo plate with a cake and set it down at the cross-roads. The fowl was set loose and the goat sent away to wander outside the village.

As I observed this ceremony the ancient Hebrew practice of sending a goat away into the wilderness, the scapegoat bearing the sins of the people, came irresistibly to mind. This might be regarded as magic, using superstitious practices to deal with problems that had other causes. Or was it? Did it not have psychological value, in word and action, putting burdens on another subject and directing the sufferer to a more hopeful future? Like many rituals, there was a purpose of care and deliverance, behind words and actions that may seem to be questionable.

Students of African religion tend to regard it in diverse ways. Either it is magic and moonshine, or it is mystical and occult. The magic is everywhere and generally less impressive than a scapegoat ritual. Houses and shops, villages and fields, seek protection from evils by hanging lucky or offensive charms in prominent places. To a critical outsider the bunches of leaves or feathers, of porcupine quills or ratskins, may seem to be useless, unless the would-be thief believes in the magic and is deterred. The Christian who disbelieves in the protective charm hanging over a shop doorway may be a more successful thief.

'Magic demands, religion implores', is a useful tag. Magic tries to control impersonal forces, by command and imitative action, and if the correct procedure is followed the result should be certain, like switching on electricity. But personal religion depends upon a spirit which has a greater and possibly contrary will to that of the suppliant, and the true word of religion is 'thy will be done'.

It might be hoped that with the development of education and modern life magic would wither away, and religion be purified into moral monotheism. But magic seems to resist or change shapes, when the old gods disappear. The prevalence of astrology and many forms of occult practice in Europe and America is proof that magic has great survival powers.

Missionaries thundered against the African idols, and a few of them tried to study the religion and its causes. Then anthropologists came to study rituals and social organization, but they seemed to think that all religion, including Christianity, was an illusion. Only a few had the sympathetic attitude of the social anthropologist Evans-Pritchard, who said that while the unbeliever seeks for some theory to explain, and explain away, the illusion, 'the believer seeks rather to understand the manner in which a people conceives of a reality and their relations to it'.[4]

The personal and deeper elements of religion are difficult to estimate. No doubt there have been thinkers in Africa, as in other continents, who have tried to pierce the secrets of the universe and who have speculated on the nature of the divine and the purpose of the human. Unhappily the absence of writing has meant that their thoughts were unrecorded and

[4] *Theories of Primitive Religion*, 1965, p. 121.

limited to tribal areas. Much of the externals of African religion seems formal, social and repetitive, 'danced out, rather than thought out'. But every dance has a purpose and there are priests and devotees to ensure that action is not meaningless.

To write of mysticism in African religion might seem absurd, but not to those who have studied ecstasy and possession, and who regard 'the seizure of man by divinity' as the most profound of all religious experiences and one which is universal. If mysticism is defined not as merely mysterious, occult or esoteric, but as 'union with God', or with a supernatural power, then there is plenty of evidence of its presence in Africa.

Many African men and women have been thought, and thought themselves, to be possessed by divine or ancestral spirits. Companies of ecstatic mediums have been widely organized in West Africa, though here and elsewhere the ecstasy may have begun as a personal experience. In old Dahomey it was said that the god 'entered the head' or 'mounted the head' of the servant that he had chosen. Here and in neighbouring Nigeria and Ghana the union of deity and human being was thought to be so close that the medium was called 'the wife of the god', whether it was a male or female medium. Early writers imagined such god-wives to be involved in sexual misconduct, and imagined heathen orgies, but the imagery of the marriage of human and divine was used in Africa as in other lands. The wife of the god received his messages and passed them on to inquirers who had come for guidance in trouble.

Possession by a divinity may occur spontaneously or be encouraged from childhood, since it is often regarded as an experience which anyone may enjoy. The ecstasy does not happen by chance, but it is encouraged by drums and songs, and by the dances of older ecstatics. In some places women, usually, though men participate also, go into states of possession for several hours, during which they may shake or dance, sing or prophesy. In other places at the first possession the person falls down as if dead, and there may be a ritual of death and resurrection, in which the novice emerges as a new personality, as I have described elsewhere.

African possessions have been interpreted as 'hysterical dissociation' or 'psychical troubles'. But careful observers have noted that they are not usually sick or badly adjusted persons, like hysterics in Europe or America. They do not try to escape from the world, since African religion is life-affirming, but they go into a trance deliberately, in time, to have communion with a god and to bring messages to inquirers. Like spiritualistic mediums in other lands, or like Islamic dervishes or Christian charismatics, African ecstatics do not generally appear to be abnormal or hysterical people in daily life, but go about their work like other people.

Whether ecstatics offer messages that come from their unconscious minds is a question of interpretation. Some writers have suggested that the mediums do not 'really' believe their own words because the experiences they describe are patently absurd. But that supernatural experiences are claimed, and believed in, is apparent from many records, as are the honesty and sincerity of the people involved. African mediums are not isolated individuals, but they interpret the beliefs of communities and they are often attached to priests and temples, so that the beliefs of the whole must be taken into account.

The ecstatics claim to have experiences which may be described as mystical, union with the divinity. But visions, dreams, even trances, may be experienced by ordinary people and the records of new prophetic religions and churches show that such experiences are widespread, today as in the past in Africa. In that past, and outside literate communities, studies of the religious experiences of the 'average' man or woman are unfortunately lacking, because of the absence of documents. There are no religious autobiographies, such as are available in literate religions, to show what the faith was like from the inside. But just as in other countries researches have revealed that religious experiences are very common, so it must have been in Africa. The experiences of the specialist may be called mystical if they indicate union with the divine, and at a less dramatic level it is probable that ordinary African believers have had religious experiences that have helped them through the troubles and strains of life.

The experiences of the past have been transformed in a new environment, and descriptions of modern movements help to provide understanding of pre-literate days. The religious services of Manyanos, Christian 'Mothers' in South Africa have been well described: 'Gradually, the audience begins to warm up. Here and there, women begin to sigh or weep softly, until one will start shaking violently in preparation for the moment when "she is taken by the Spirit" and begins to speak. The other women listen intently, in close participation, and while the speaker slowly works herself up to a high pitch of emotion, the feelings of the listeners find in her a channel through which they pour themselves out, and by so doing generate again renewed tension in the individual who acts as a focus of, and outlet for, the collective mood . . . all the emotions find their release like so many tumultuous rivulets joining together and reaching the tranquillity of a broad flowing river'.[5]

[5] M. Brandel-Syrier, *Black Woman in Search of God*, 1962, p. 34f.

Chapter Twelve

AFRICAN CHANGE

Africa in the Bible?

A conference was held at the Hebrew University in Jerusalem on 'Africa and the Bible', with African clergy who knew about their continent, Jewish scholars who knew about the Bible, and a few observers who had experience of both subjects. The visitors stayed at Ain Karim, a village outside Jerusalem traditionally associated with John the Baptist, and at the convent the nuns welcomed them. At a simple but substantial dinner all the other delegates were Africans, and an old student asked me, 'Are you the only coloured man here?'

At the conference some speakers had axes to grind, and it is a curious comment on the methods of the French and British empires that some of their products tended to reproduce the characteristics of their former masters. French-speaking Africans often began late, went on too long, and wove wonderful theories in flowery language, while African English-speakers would try to keep to the time and the point, be shorter and more factual.

Despite some English-speaking scepticism, it was a popular theme that Africa was in the Bible. Egypt is there, but these speakers were all black and from tropical Africa, and they fastened on names like Cush, which might have been the Sudan, and assumed from there that Biblical influence might have spread to the tropics in olden days.

From the Jewish side, there were several suggestions that there might have been contacts between Jews and Africans long ago. There were routes across the Sahara desert, before modern sea and air travel led to the neglect and abandonment of the oases. Some priests in old Ashanti had worn ornaments that resembled Jewish priestly breastplates, and the Bible might have been distributed by Jewish traders.

Criticism of these speculations caused division. Wherever Cush was, nobody could prove any link with it from tropical Africa, and what does it matter anyway since the Gospel is universal? The presence of Jewish traders in the African tropics is doubtful and without evidence, and rare similarity of dress does not prove contact. As for distributing the Bible in Africa, there is no evidence for its presence before the nineteenth century in tropical Africa, and that was the work of Christian missionaries and their converts. This critic was called a 'missionary' by an eminent Biblical scholar, though he apologized later.

A search for an ancient ancestry for African religion has been pursued by several writers, perhaps to counter the historical claims of Christianity and Islam. Most Africans believed in a supreme God long before the missionaries arrived, and the idea of life after death was everywhere.

African names and titles for God have fascinated some students, especially those who wanted to link their peoples to some ancient civilization, Hebrew, Egyptian or even Mesopotamian, and ingenious ways of doing this have been found. A common central African name for God is Lesa, and it has been dissected in this way: *sa* is claimed to be a suffix that can be dropped, *le* can be reversed to make *el*, and El or Elohim was a Hebrew name for God which could have come from the Bible to tropical Africa.

A name for God among the Ashanti of Ghana is Twi-adu-ampon, and years ago a well-known lawyer, J. B. Danquah, tried to prove its ancient and distant origin. Twi is another name for the Ashanti race and language and so he claimed that 'Twii was a corruption of the old and hallowed African ethnic name Cush', while Adu 'is a variant of Anu', and 'Anu was the name

of the God of an ancient people . . . ancient Babylonia'.[1]   An
extreme attempt to prove such a distant ancestry for African
religion was made by the African Archdeacon J. O. Lucas of
Lagos in his book *The Religion of the Yorubas*. Briefly, Lucas
considered a number of West African peoples and languages,
and concluded that 'not less than half' their language and
religion was derived from ancient Egypt. For example, a
Yoruba name for a spirit called Aroni was, suggested Lucas,
'probably the survival of a deity connected with the famous city
of On'. But the most striking effort at etymological connections
resembles the dissection of Lesa described above. The
commonest name for God among the Yoruba of Nigeria is Ol-
Orun, generally interpreted as the prefix *ol* meaning 'owner',
and *orun*, 'the sky'. Lucas looked round for an Egyptian parallel,
dropped *ol* as a mere prefix and the final *n* as a nasalization.
There remains *oru*, and what is there like it in Egypt? Why, the
great god Horus, and so Yoruba belief in God is Egyptian!

Lucas has been criticized strongly by scholars, Africans and
others, and his knowledge of the ancient Egyptian language
seems to have been as shaky as his history. But some African
historians have been attracted by theories of the migrations of
black tropical peoples from ancient centres of culture, especially
Egypt, and secondarily the ancient kingdom of Meroë on the
upper Nile. Most tribes have traditions of wandering from
other places, and there have been many migrations in all the
continents, but it is usually difficult to chart their travels and
identify places of origin with certainty. A popular Yoruba
historian claims that his people came from the east, therefore
from Mecca, Arabia, Egypt or Palestine, even identifying them
as descendants of Nimrod who was a mighty hunter in the book
of Genesis. Such speculations, generally without firm evidence,
run the danger of being accepted as fact in popular books and
newspapers.

[1] *The Akan Doctrine of God*, 1944, p. 49

Perhaps there was a feeling of inferiority, working itself out as superiority, in the search for distinguished origins, as other people compile family trees to claim descent from nobility or royalty. Many modern Europeans in Africa were offensively superior, even when they came from low social classes, claiming an ancient heritage and despising the 'untutored blacks'. The latter got their own back by tracing descent from Egypt or other cultures which flourished when the British went about in skins and painted their bodies with woad.

The study of the traditional religions of Africa is not helped by being taken as imitations of Egypt, any more than they were understood by early writers who called them the work of the devil. The eminent biographer Emil Ludwig once asked, 'How can the untutored African conceive God?' The fact is that Africans did have such subtle and significant beliefs. Theologically this might be claimed as revelation, more prosaically it is evidence of individual and communal religion stretching far back into the past, before any outside influences appeared. African religions deserve study in their own right, and their functions in society, which anthropologists have stressed, need examining more fully. In recent centuries many outside influences have appeared and they help to form the complexity of the modern African scene.

Old and New

African religions today are not all the pre-literate customs and beliefs that used to be called 'fetishism' or 'juju'. Such inaccurate and derogatory words are no longer used in scholarly books and other descriptions are sought. When a census was taken in Lagos people were asked to state whether they were Christian, Muslim or pagan. But to those city dwellers 'pagan' meant the naked tribes of the interior whom Christians and Muslims had tried in vain to clothe. Very few were returned as pagan. When a similar census was taken at Ibadan later people were asked whether they were Christian, Muslim or animist. But few knew what 'animist' meant and again ignored the question.

Most inhabitants of the big cities of Africa would be called Christians or Muslims, whether or not they ever attended church or mosque. They would be potential or adhering members, or their children would attend a religious school. It is one of the great changes of this century that Africa has largely changed from being a 'sea of paganism', into a continent where two major historical and literate religions run side by side, Islam and Christianity. Islam is strongest in the north, the Mediterranean countries, Christianity mostly in the tropical and southern regions. Statistics are very general but in the mid-eighties it is reckoned that there are 200 million Christians in Africa, 190 million Muslims, and 60 million adhering to 'tribal' or 'traditional' religions. For Christianity it is one of the greatest successes of modern times, since at the beginning of the century the numbers of Christians, including the old Coptic churches of Egypt and Ethiopia, would not have been reckoned at much more than 10 million for the whole continent.

The attitudes of the early Christian missionaries to the traditional religions of Africa was incomprehension and condemnation, they were the work of the Devil or religions of fear. Even African converts, such as Samuel Ajayi Crowther (1806–1891), the first Anglican African bishop, spoke of African religion as 'Satan's tool'. His mother had been a priestess of the Yoruba god Obatala, but young Ajayi had been taken as a slave at the age of fifteen and then rescued by a British warship and taken to Sierra Leone where he was baptized. Later ordained he had a strong evangelical impulse to his own people, but in practice he advised his agents to be cautious and tolerant. He discussed religious beliefs and practices with village chiefs, and gave detailed accounts of traditional rituals, and he was not so derogatory in accounts of them as European missionaries often were.

Later missionaries who began to take an interest in African religions were still ready to seek out the Devil. Farrow among the Yoruba wrote of 'Objects of belief—the Devil', and Basden among the Igbo said that 'eternally opposed to God is His arch-enemy "Ekwensu" (the Devil) whose one purpose is to frustrate the goodness of God and to disseminate evil'. Modern research has shown that Ekwensu is a spirit of violence, which was usefully invoked by warriors and hunters. Present studies of African religions have been undertaken largely by anthropologists, but there have been great missionary pioneers, such as Edwin W. Smith in his classic work on the Ila-speaking Peoples of Northern Rhodesia (Zambia). Other missionaries and African Christians have benefited by such studies and the general result is that of more tolerant understanding of the ancient religions, though there is a tendency by foreign workers to ignore these studies and concentrate on their tasks of administration or education.

Towards Islam also the attitude of Christian missionaries was hostility or ignorance in Africa. The end of Bishop Crowther's life was saddened by conflict with a new generation of young missionaries. Part of the Keswick evangelical movement, they went to Africa with the slogan 'convert the world in one generation'. (How many times has one heard that? It is the cry of modern 'born again Christians', with naive conversion schemes backed up by modern technology). These new young missionaries thought that the Muslim tribes of the interior of Africa were 'superior' to the negroes of the coast where Crowther worked with most success. They criticized him for being too easy-going with his agents, and for lack of success among the Muslims. One said that Crowther emphasized the 'non-spiritual benefits' of his mission when talking to Muslim rulers, and that in seven palavers with them Crowther had only once mentioned the blood of Christ and never the life after death.

Crowther was unusually diplomatic in relations with

Muslims and speaking of one he said, 'I introduce myself to him as a mallam sent by the great mallams of the white man's country, to see the state of the heathen population, and to know the mind of the rulers, whether we might teach the people the religion of the Ansara (Nazarene).' He was allowed to work among the non-Muslim population and this approach proved the most useful.

Crowther practised toleration and employed Muslim interpreters, translating the Bible and compiling dictionaries in several languages. Late in life he wrote, 'I knew thirty years ago that Mohammedans are not easily converted to Christianity. . . . Yet I know that Christians can live and associate with Mohammedans as friends, and share in the conversion of the heathen to the worship of the one true God'.

Speaking of the Koran he said, 'I am not prejudiced against it, but read it, and compare its doctrine with that of our Bible, that I may know the difference between them, and which teaches the best religion.' He remarked later that since Gabriel, who is mentioned in the Koran, referred in the Bible to Mary's child as the Son of God, there was 'undeniable' proof of this doctrine, despite Muslim rejection. This was not likely to prove acceptable but Crowther urged that the Bible should be translated into Arabic and Hausa, and said that Christians should 'not dispute about the truth or falsehood of one religion or the other, but we should aim at toleration'.

There was been very little Christian success in converting Muslims, and vice versa, but at least there is the possibility of better understanding in view of the many scholarly studies that have been made of Islam. There have been some Roman Catholic and Protestant attempts at placing missionaries in Muslim cities, not with the aim of conversion but of understanding practices and ways of life. Learning Arabic and studying the Koran are essentials, just as Christians recommend the study of the Bible in other languages.

Dangers of Success

Christianity has made greater advances in Africa than in any other continent in modern times, and while its support or practice may have declined in Europe or America its increase in Africa implies a greater participation of Africans in world Christian affairs and teaching.

Modern success undoubtedly owed much to the protection of colonial governments, but this could have unfortunate effects. Roman Catholic reformers speak now of the adverse results of authoritarian rule in their church, and the dangers of triumphalism, but the same might be said of all churches in Africa: Roman Catholic, Anglican, Methodist, Baptist, and the rest.

The missionary, like the colonial officer, was in a position of unchallenged authority, and even when exercising it benevolently his superiority was manifest. Mary Kingsley, who travelled on her own among cannibal tribes in the eighteen nineties, admired some missionaries, like Mary Slessor of Calabar, but she preferred the company of traders, sailors and her own cannibal Fans. She criticized missionaries for interfering unnecessarily with social customs. They made their female converts wear Mother Hubbards, long overalls, because they disliked seeing bare breasts, thereby revealing their own complexes. They often stopped people's amusements, regarding dancing as immoral and diabolical, and often destroying their drums.

Such authoritarianism had strange results. The missionaries condemned polygamy as heathen, although it is in the Old Testament, and they tried to impose Christian marriage with very little success. By Christian marriage they meant weddings in church, conducted by a minister, and in this even evangelical Protestants were unconsciously following the decrees of the Counter-Reformation Council of Trent. In earlier Christian practice marriage could be celebrated anywhere, a priest was not necessary, and secular customs were accepted since marriage is a social contract and not exclusively Christian.

Baptism was refused to polygamists almost everywhere in Africa, and only Bishop Colenso of Natal (1851) thought that they could be baptized. Bishop Crowther disagreed, as did other missionaries, but he allowed the wives of polygamists to be baptized which was more than some missionaries permitted. He was firm but understanding on polygamy, saying, 'I do not condone it . . . but I understand it. Even some of my own native teachers have returned to it. They have their arguments and sometimes it is difficult to refute them.' Yet he emphasized the subordinate position of the women in a polygamous household and paraphrased a Yoruba proverb which said that 'no woman would ever undertake the expense of making a sacrifice to please her god in order that her husband may take a second wife'.

Others were more severe. In Nigeria a man who was converted to Christianity had two wives. It was decreed that he must send one away, the younger, which might have led her into prostitution and he refused to do this. So he was denied baptism, and his wives and children also. None could become communicants, though they had accepted the Christian faith and remained loyal worshippers at the village church and its principal financial support. The appeal of Islam, which allows a man four legal wives, may be appreciated.

Virtually all mission churches had strict systems of discipline, which they practised with a rigidity that would have caused rebellion in a European church. There were often members 'under discipline', who had to sit at the back of the church, for trivial offences such as wearing a charm necklace or drinking beer. A man 'under discipline', though a church member, might be refused baptism to his children even if his wife was in good standing. This was virtual excommunication, even in churches that rarely celebrated the sacrament and had a low view of its importance. 'They do not deserve Communion frequently', one remarked, as if any of us do.

The authoritarian structure of the churches was a strength in a sea of disorganized paganism, though it cut people off from their own traditions. Where there were separate Christian villages it almost detribalized them. It helped to build the churches up to their present great numbers, but it had serious weaknesses which time is revealing. It led to vainglory among its leaders, where the merest young lay missionary could be more powerful than traditional bishops at home, and gain an overweening sense of his own importance. Churches that had repudiated the Papacy developed a similar sense of their own orthodoxy and infallibility, and regarded their own views on marriage as unquestionable.

Such imperialist rule was reinforced by the superiority of colour. Missionaries were white, and when there were African priests and pastors they were in the second rank. In French colonies, which are wrongly supposed to have had no colour bar, it was the regular practice to call all Africans, even their clergy, 'tu' and 'toi', the familiar 'thou' form which in France is reserved for children and servants.

The role played by African agents, catechists, teachers, and pastors, has been greatly underestimated, for without them the church could not have succeeded. The missionary lived away from the people, in a fine house, and often did not speak the language of the country, so that he was completely dependent upon his African agents. Yet they were directly engaged in promoting Christianity, by word and life. There is a great deal of research still to be done into the activities and the writings of these lay African workers.

The practice of Crowther is interesting again. He believed in the conversion of Africa by Africans, but in the nineteenth century there were too few Nigerian Christians to engage in evangelization, so a Native Pastorate was established with

Africans from Sierra Leone. They had a higher standard of living than most of the people among whom they worked, but lower than that of Europeans, and this would be justified by the claim that they brought not only Christianity but Civilization and western ways of dress and life.

Crowther's Native Agents were paid less than European missionaries, and they seem to have adapted to the conditions of life more easily, for malaria and yellow and black fever were still killing many Europeans, often within a few weeks of arrival in the country. Accusations were made against some of these agents of dishonesty or engaging in trade, and immorality (often only on hearsay), and Crowther was considered to be too lenient in discipline. But the wonder is that these agents, and the native Nigerians who succeeded them, worked so faithfully. Conditions were appallingly difficult, and they themselves were often only recent converts to Christianity.

In emphasizing the African character of the mission Crowther was following the far-sighted policy of the Rev Henry Venn, honorary clerical secretary of the Church Missionary Society from 1841–1872. He deliberately planned the formation of 'Native Churches' and a 'Native Pastorate'. European missionaries would start by preaching the Gospel, but as congregations were formed, with the indispensable help of African interpreters, they would be maintained by catechists and the missionary would move on to evangelize another area. He even foresaw a time when 'the Episcopate must be native and raised up from among themselves'. The Society should not send out 'Missionary Bishops', but wait until indigenous congregations produced their own, so that 'the Episcopate should be Native rather than European'.

Crowther provided the ideal example for Venn's policy and he persisted with this plan, so that a special Bill was put through Parliament to allow for the creation of a new bishopric on the Niger, 'in the countries in Western Africa beyond the limit of her Majesty's dominions', in other words, outside the colonial area of Sierra Leone which already had its own European bishop. Crowther was given an honorary D.D. at Oxford and was consecrated bishop in Canterbury Cathedral in 1864.

There was opposition from the start. A missionary, Henry Townsend at Abeokuta, wrote to Venn: 'A native episcopate is one of those fancies that need only to be realized, put to the test, to prove a disappointment.' And again, 'the extraordinary expense of the Niger Mission conducted by Natives alone shows what they can do if the purse is placed in their hands.' Crowther himself had refused the honour at first, saying that the missionaries had 'sacrificed everything', and 'as a man I know the feeling of men. . . . The plan of placing a Native in a higher position where Europeans have to take part in the same field is very premature.'

Crowther had a long and honourable episcopate, but he came to be regarded as an exception, if not a mistake. After Venn's death there was a change of mission policy. Inspectors were sent out to Africa who criticized the mission as not having 'a high tone of Christian life', or lacking in 'Pentecostal blessing'. With little experience, they criticized the 'negro character' and said the people were 'very like boys to deal with'. There was a long struggle, and the Niger mission was divided into European and African missionary spheres. From the death of Crowther in 1891 there was no other African diocesan bishop under the Church Missionary Society until 1953. His successors were Europeans, with Africans only as assistant bishops. Only since 1953 have there been African bishops and a full measure of independence in this and other African churches.

A note may be added on the use of the word 'native'. This came in recent years to be regarded as derogatory and 'indigene' was often substitited. On the French side 'indigène' was thought to be improper, and 'natif' was substituted.

Independency

Harsh authority may provoke reaction, even among 'untutored' peoples. For various reasons: discipline, polygamy, personality clash, or desire for more colourful and emotional religion, there have been many schisms and separations in African Christianity. These are mostly among Protestants, some among Roman Catholics but fewer because their rigid structure encouraged less activity by lay leaders and priestly dogmatism repeated the old claim, 'outside the church no salvation'.

These separatists or sectarians, or Independents to give them a respectable title with a tradition of self-government, have sprung up all over tropical and southern Africa. It has been estimated that there are over six thousand independent African church organizations. Of course schisms and multiplicity of churches are not only features of African Christian life, they have occurred widely in other continents. The divisions of European churches are ageold, and in America their number is legion. Indeed some of the African independents were influenced by American negro or evangelical organizations, though most of them are purely African and testify to the vigour and independence of Africans.

Critics of the Independents often claimed that their motives were unworthy or immoral, the leaders wanting to have many wives. Or they were troublemakers (*mauvais esprits*) because they had fallen out with missionaries. Doing some research on *Religion in an African City*, for the University College of Ibadan, it was soon found that polygamy was only a minor motive for secession, and not all the Independents permitted it. The chief stimulus to secession was religious experience, fed by visions and dreams, which led to revival movements. When the official church tried to check this revival there was often a schism. On their side the separatists accused the mother church of formalism, 'quenching the Spirit'. There was a link here with the traditional religions, in which priests and prophets, mediums and ecstatics, were inspired and gave new messages. In the Christian context these messages were scriptural, for the Independents are strongly Biblical and it is rare that they have new or 'heretical' doctrines.

One of the best known mass movements to Christianity came with the preaching of a Grebo prophet in Liberia, William Wadé Harris in 1913. He travelled through the French Ivory Coast and is said to have baptized 120,000 people before being deported by the French colonial government which suspected sedition, especially as he was not ordained and preached in English. He had great effect, even through interpreters one of whom, Victor Tano, helped me in interpretation twenty years later. After a long wait for help from the missions, about half the converts were received into the Methodist church, but the independent Harrist church today still numbers some 200,000 adult and affiliated members.

In the Congo in 1921 a great Christian movement was led by the prophet Simon Kimbangu. He was thrown into prison by the Belgian authorities and remained there almost till his death, but his movement spread and became one of the largest independent churches in Africa, with over five million adherents. Long viewed with suspicion by some missionaries, the 'Church of Jesus Christ on Earth through the Prophet Simon Kimbangu' was admitted to the World Council of Churches in 1969, though most African independents remain outside that organization or comparable local bodies.

In South Africa one of the most remarkable of thousands of independent churches is the Zulu Ama Nazaretha, or Nazarites, founded by the prophet Isaiah Shembe in 1911. His church, which has retained more traditional customs than many, has been described by the Swedish Bishop Sundkler in *Bantu Prophets in South Africa*.

Although there is great variety among the independent churches, they are in general remarkable for their combination of Christian faith with African outlook, inspiration by prophetic and charismatic leaders, and often for the foundation of religious communities which have high standards of morality. Critics warn of the 'syncretism' of African and Christian beliefs, forgetting that Christianity is a syncretism of Hebrew and Greek elements, and that European and American churches are often far removed from the practices and beliefs of the first Christians.

Persecution has tried African Christians, in the foundation of their churches in the last two centuries, and reappears today. In Uganda there have been notable examples of courage and heroism. In February 1977 the Anglican bishops of Uganda sent a letter to President Amin saying, among other things, that 'Christians are asking, If this is what is happening to our bishops, then where are we? The gun whose muzzle has been pressed against the Archbishop's stomach, the gun used to search the Bishop of Bukedi's house, is a gun pointed at every Christian in the church.' Within days Archbishop Luwum was killed, and other priests and ordinary Christians were murdered openly or disappeared.

It is clear that Christianity has taken root in Africa. It may not be our church organization, but it is the same Christian faith that Europeans received from overseas. Africans have taken the Bible to themselves and it has become their scripture and language classic. African spiritual life, with prophets and dreams, is original and impressive. African spiritual and moral guidance, and courage in the face of tyranny, are an example to the world. Dictatorial regimes will not kill the faith, for that has been proved already with Simon Kimbangu, Janani Luwum, and many others.

Chapter Thirteen

CHRISTIAN SYNTHESES

Black Virgin

Every day before dawn dark-skinned pilgrims throng into the basilica of Guadalupe to adore the Black Virgin. Guadalupe was once a village to the north of Mexico City, but is now a suburb swamped into the sprawling town which claims a population of twelve million, one of the world's largest cities. Visitors come from all over Latin America to its most famous shrine here.

The modern basilica is a great circular concrete structure, over which rises a pointed copper roof. Strips of copper were still being rapidly nailed on when I was there in 1976, and everywhere feverish activity tried to complete the work before the great anniversary on the Sunday. Inside there is a plain altar and rostrum, with a forest of man-size candles, and from the roof hang clusters of lights like Chinese lanterns. The building is always crowded with worshippers, dark Indians, coloured half-castes and lighter Spanish, and a succession of masses continues all day, from five in the morning till eight at night.

Many worshippers come to this church on their knees, and many have pads to protect their knees over the distances. Families kneel down at the courtyard gates and shuffle on their knees up to the building and over the concrete floor towards the altar. Some come kneeling from longer distances in special acts of penance or intercession, and half-ruined monuments mark the stages on the road from the city.

Behind the altar hangs the object of pilgrimage, the Black Virgin of Guadalupe. It is a mild and gracious picture, with shining robes, undoubtedly a dark figure but in sharp contrast to the fierce or abstract sculptures of ancient Mexican gods. To this picture pilgrims come to kneel and pray, and many would like to stay in front of it all day. To avoid traffic jams of kneeling suppliants the ingenious architects and clerics of the new basilica have devised a moving floor, or rather four strips of floor, with chromium hand rails as on underground escalators. The devotees enter their pen, kneel to the Virgin and are slowly moved along, turning their heads as they go, till the next batch of worshippers presses on to the moving floor. Only the Roman church could have conceived such an arrangement, but perhaps only that church could so have captured the hearts of Mexican Indians.

The basilica of the Black Virgin is both ostentatious and impressive. Coming to it after visiting monuments of ancient Mexico at Teotihuacan to the north, with their cold and cruel splendour, here is the air of real devotion. At the anniversary of the shrine all the surrounding roads are packed with hundreds of thousands of pilgrims. Those groups that can force their way through dance up to the holy picture and round the church, dancing rather than praying, in traditional fashion and costumes.

Vast courtyards, with strong metal and wire fences, surround the new basilica. At the back is the old shrine, a baroque eighteenth century church, which is now closed. Like many Mexican edifices it was built with little foundation and is slowly sinking into the ground. A seminary next to it is lop-sided and looks as if it might fall over at any minute. Behind rises the hill where the vision appeared that gave rise to the cult and the churches.

It was in December 1531, barely ten years after the fall of Mexico City to the Spaniards, that an Indian peasant claimed that he saw the Virgin Mary here. It is said that she had appeared previously some miles away, but when Juan Diego was climbing this hill the Virgin appeared to him among the rocks. She called him 'my son', and told him to charge the bishop to build a shrine so that she might watch over the Indians. The bishop was sceptical, as such gentlemen often are, and the vision came twice more until Diego was given a sign to prove authenticity. The Virgin told him to gather roses among the rocks, wrap them in his serape cloth, and take them to the bishop. When he opened the cloth before the bishop it was stamped with the picture of the Black Virgin. This is said to be the picture which hangs above the altar at Guadalupe, and it is reproduced in countless copies and found in churches and houses all over central America.

Most towns of any size in Mexico have a church of Guadalupe, with a picture of the famous relic. Over ninety per cent of Mexicans are said to be Roman Catholics, and the cult of the Black Virgin undoubtedly helped to give the new faith deep roots in the country.

Conquistadores

The arrival of the Spaniards in Mexico in the sixteenth century was a bold and savage invasion, with a gross mixture of religion, greed and treachery. Some historians have suggested that at the Crusades European rulers were glad to get rid of mercenary soldiers, violent bandits, and restless younger sons by sending them anywhere away from home to make their fortunes or be killed. Similarly perhaps Spain was glad to get rid of its trigger-happy adventurers into the fortunately discovered outlet of the New World. Who would want to keep Cortés or Pizarro at home, if they could wreak their lust for gain far away?

Bernal Díaz, the last survivor of the conquerors of Mexico, described in his old age the overthrow of the Aztec empire in his graphic and revealing *Conquest of New Spain*. A few hundred Spaniards, with horses and guns, fought their way along the Mexican coast, climbed into the interior mountains, marched on Mexico City, were first expelled and later returned to capture and destroy the capital and empire. Throughout all this there is a mixture of violence and religion that astonishes the modern reader.

The Aztecs themselves were a conquering people, like the Romans, who had subjugated more civilized peoples whose great pyramids and temples were the shrines of Maya, Nahua, Toltec and other races. With their captives the Aztecs practised human sacrifice, both because it would have been dangerous to keep large numbers of prisoners and for religious reasons. These were sacrifices to their sun god, which was supposed to be kept firmly in the sky by the great numbers of victims. A great temple pyramid which they built in Mexico City was completed with the sacrifice of twenty thousand people.

When they arrived in Mexico City the Spaniards were impressed with the splendour of the buildings. 'We did not know what to say, or if this was real that we saw before our eyes. On the land side there were great cities, and on the lake many more. At intervals along the causeway there were many bridges, and before us was the great city of Mexico. As for us, we were scarcely four hundred strong.'

It was a current belief that the white men were ancestors or saviours, whose coming had been foretold to the Mexicans. The emperor Montezuma told the Spaniards, 'that we must truly be the men about whom his ancestors had long ago prophesied, saying that they would come from the direction of the sunrise to rule over these lands.' By clever strategy the Spaniards took Montezuma captive at gunpoint, but during their retreat under attack from the Mexican armies Montezuma was hit by three stones and died. Díaz says that Cortés and all his captains wept for Montezuma and mourned him as a father, and 'the best king they ever had in Mexico'.

The Spaniards were out for booty, especially gold which they found in abundance in Mexico and Peru, but they also had their ideology and tried to convert the Mexicans to Christianity. Cortés himself preached to Montezuma saying, according to Díaz, 'that we were Christians and worshipped one God alone, named Jesus Christ, who had suffered his passion and death to save us; and that what they worshipped as gods were not gods but devils, which were evil things, and if they were ugly to look at, their deeds were uglier.' Montezuma replied more tolerantly, 'we have worshipped our own gods here from the beginning and know them to be good. No doubt yours are good also, but do not trouble to tell us any more about them at present.'

The Spaniards told the Aztecs to destroy their idols, but wanted to replace them with images of Christ and the Virgin Mary. They were shocked at the human sacrifices of the Aztecs, but their own deeds brought massacres and destruction. They had the Inquisition at home, and after the conquest they used its methods to torture Mexicans and force them into submission. One of the friars urged Cortés to restrain his zeal, but the Aztec empire was utterly destroyed, its glory as well as its cruelty, and replaced by a mixture of splendour and poverty from an alien culture.

Christianity went hand in glove with military conquest in Mexico, Peru and many other parts of America. Some of the clergy dominated the people, but others lived near and with them. They were often defenders of the poor against the oppression of soldiers and landlords, as they are in liberation movements in Latin America today. What little remains of literature about the old religion was largely preserved through the Christian missionaries, even though they did not believe in it.

Whether the story of the Black Virgin was a masterly invention of priestly strategy, or the beginnings of Indian faith, it provided a basis for the new religion. Graham Greene, in an account of visiting Guadalupe in *The Lawless Roads*, remarks that it may be doubted whether the average Spaniard would have thought that an Indian should be addressed by the Virgin as 'my son', and priests would have been more inclined to emphasize the superiority of the church and white Madonnas.

This was a Black Virgin for Indians, who was said to love Indians, and that restored their self-respect and gave them a faith of their own which still endures.

In the nineteen twenties President Calles of Mexico tried to break the power of the church and destroy the faith of the people, persecuting Christianity with the zeal of Cortés against the Aztec religion. Many priests were expelled or shot, among them Miguel Pro, the original of the whisky priest of Greene's novel *The Power and the Glory*, who was shot a year and a half after his arrival in the country. In some provinces all the churches were destroyed or closed, but then the people erected the altars again and priests and bishops returned.

The shrine of Guadalupe remained open even at the height of the persecution. No government was able to rob the Indians of their Virgin, and this shrine helped to break the career of the only man who threatened it. When the dictator of Tabasco, Garrido Canabal, arrived in Mexico City he gave private orders that the shrine was to be destroyed, as he had already sacked the churches in Tabasco province. But the basilica of the Black Virgin was guarded day and night and came to no harm, while Garrido was eventually driven from Mexico into exile in Costa Rica.

At the hill where the Virgin appeared at Guadalupe it is said that there was an ancient Mexican sanctuary. Perhaps the shrine is one of Montezuma's revenges. Or it may be that the more things change, the more they are the same.

This is one example of a Christian synthesis, and there are countless others, illustrating many beliefs and methods of conversion. The next example is selected both for its topical interest, and again because of personal involvement.

Moonies

An invitation arrived to 'The Fifth International Conference for the Unity of the Sciences', to be held at the Washington Hilton

Hotel, Washington D.C. The Chairman of the conference would be Sir John Eccles, Nobel Laureate, and the theme 'The Search for Absolute Values; Harmony among the Sciences'. The conference was sponsored by an International Cultural Foundation, which would pay fees and expenses. The academic respectability of the foundation seemed to be guaranteed by distinguished figures who were taking part, but when the formal invitation followed it appeared that the founder of the International Cultural Foundation was Sun Myung Moon.

There had been adverse rumours about this man. BBC television gave a programme to the Moon church, stating that Mr Moon had been claimed as Messiah though noting that it had no evidence that he himself made such a claim. Some of his disciples were said to have been brain-washed, though again no evidence was available. *The Observer* newspaper described a London representative of this church as a sinister young man and noted that before his interview he bowed his head in prayer for a few minutes and this seemed to be dangerous.

Professor Kenneth Mellanby, an eminent scientist and my former principal at the University College of Ibadan, wrote an article for the scientific journal *Nature* on a 'Moon conference' and stated 'Here we had a gathering of good men and women with good minds, who seriously discussed the problems facing, the world today, and the ways in which science could and should be involved. I know of no other gathering where this would have been possible. . . . We did not solve all the world's outstanding problems, but perhaps we made some progress in the right direction.'

The *New York Times* reported that Mr Moon and his Unification Church had been accused of anti-Semitism and two American rabbis said that Mr Moon had interpreted the Holocaust of Jews in Nazi Germany as divine punishment for the Crucifixion of Jesus. But Professor Richard Rubinstein, himself a Jew, had attended a Moon conference and rejected such charges. He stated that some conservative Christians share this view of the Holocaust, and some orthodox Jewish rabbis also interpret it as divine punishment, and both do it not from hatred but from faith in God acting in history. He himself rejected these opinions but thought it unfair to single out Mr Moon for expressing a belief that many Christians and Jews affirm.

Dr Alan Nixon of the American Chemical Society wrote to the journal *Science* which had reported 'a peculiar emptiness in the eyes of many Moon followers'. Dr Nixon retorted, 'I talked with a lot of the young people there. I found them attractive, with adequate intelligence (perhaps not up to the standard demanded by the Editors of *Science*) and apparently happy with what they were doing.' What really worried opponents of the Moonies 'was the fact that so many young people were joining the Unification Church and that this was breaking up homes'. But Dr Nixon remarked that in America adolescence is prolonged by sheltering children more than in other countries. A court ruling in San Francisco gave five young members of the Moonie church back into the custody of their parents, a ruling that was later suspended as a violation of constitutional rights of freedom of worship. The 'young people' were aged between 21 and 26.

The *Washington Post* wrote that Mr Moon and his chief advisor had figured in a federal investigation of South Korean 'influence-buying' in the United States, and remarked that none of the participants in a conference 'seemed troubled by the fact that it was Moon who brought them together nor did they seem terribly concerned about what his motives might be'. But some attended these conferences precisely to find out what Mr Moon was like, what his ideas were, how the movement was funded, what support it had, and if there were deeper influences behind it. Many participants, like many young Moonies themselves, left the conferences or the movement when they had fuller information, and this abandonment must have been accelerated after Mr Moon had been convicted in the courts of tax evasion and sentenced to prison.

At the beginning of the conference there was a reception at which Mr Moon and his wife welcomed the delegates. He gave the impression of being more of a business man than a charismatic leader, but orientals are difficult to assess. There was a lavish teetotal buffet, and easy meeting of scholars and friends from many countries. At the opening of the conference Mr Moon gave a Founder's Address on the universe and man, the family and love, and the importance of absolute values. It was not particularly scientific or philosophical, but it was not propagandist.

A surprising feature of this conference was the absence of literature or propaganda from Mr Moon's church. This was different from some conferences where there are many leaflets and books from the sponsoring bodies. Dr Nixon commented, 'when I asked them for some literature explaining the origin, philosophy and activities of the church they had none available.' Such reserve might suggest reluctance to reveal material to critical eyes. Conferences for 'the Unity of the Sciences' might in themselves be propaganda, covers for deeper activities, but they were very expensive ways of working, and where did the money come from?

Some time later, in response to numerous requests from scholars who had attended conferences of the International Cultural Foundation, three seminars were held. These were at Puerto Rico, Alicante in Spain, and Hawaii, always in the best hotels, for those who could attend from nearby countries. Lectures were given by the secretary-general, Sun Myung Moon's religious and political ideas were expounded, and free and frank discussion followed, in which it may be said that very few accepted the Moonie teaching.

Divine Principle

At these seminars for the first time copies of *Divine Principle* were distributed, the scripture or new revelation of the Unification Church. It bears no author's name but the General Introduction claims that 'with the fullness of time, God has sent His messenger to resolve the fundamental questions of life and the universe. His name is Sun Myung Moon . . . He endured suffering unimagined by anyone in human history . . . He fought alone against myriads of Satanic forces, both in the spiritual and physical worlds, and finally triumphed over them all. In this way he came in contact with many saints in Paradise and with Jesus, and thus brought to light all the heavenly secrets through his communion with God.'

The relationship of this church to other Christian bodies is confusing. The original name of the movement, still printed on the title page of *Divine Principle*, was 'The Holy Spirit Association for the Unification of World Christianity'. But if there was once an aim of uniting the churches from within, it seems to have been dropped with the development of the Unification Church in its own right, becoming a new religious organization like the Mormons or Christian Science.

To some extent the Unification Church seems to be Christian-Buddhist synthesis, a by-product of Christian missionary work in Korea but outside its organizations, like prophetic and independent churches in other lands. The Bible is often quoted, sometimes literally and sometimes figuratively. Thus Adam and Eve are held to have really existed, as the parents of mankind, but the Second Coming in the clouds is figurative, though both are important in the scheme of the *Divine Principle*.

It is asserted that God has 'dual characteristics' and so has mankind, with male and female elements from Adam and Eve onwards. The Buddhist concept is quoted of the dualism of Sung-sang and Hyung-sang in Korean, like the Chinese Yin and

Yang. Our first parents fell by being 'tempted by the archangel Lucifer into illicit and forbidden love'. Perfection will come with the unity of mankind, in which the family has central importance. Sun Myung Moon has held mass weddings of couples chosen by himself in several countries, to emphasize this male-female unity.

Unification theology teaches that Jesus came to restore mankind to God, but he was rejected and crucified. Also he was not married. The Second Coming of Christ is affirmed, but with an ingenious variation on Adventism that has not appeared elsewhere. It is said that as at his first coming Christ did not appear on the clouds, as was expected, but was born into a human family, so will the Second Coming be. This is put succinctly in *Unification Theological Affirmations*: 'Christ will come as before, as a man in the flesh, and he will establish a family through marriage to his Bride, a woman in the flesh, and they will become the True Parents of mankind.' Support for this is found in the woman and child to come in Revelation 12.

Belief in the human and married Christ seems to point to Sun Myung Moon, a married man with ten children. In an interview given to *Newsweek International* Mr Moon, when asked whether he was the Messiah, replied, 'Let God answer you, let God answer the world'. However, some of his followers seemed to expect him to be declared Messiah. It is said that there were 2,000 years from Adam to Abraham, 2,000 from Abraham to Jesus, and 2,000 from then till now.

The centrality of Sun Myung Moon is reinforced by the prominence given to Korea, the land of his birth, which with Japan and the U.S.A. has the largest numbers of Moon followers. Korea is said to be the meeting-place of religions, though India, Iran or Israel might be more so. But to *Newsweek* Mr Moon declared, 'Korea is the chosen nation of God. Korea is divided. The line-up in Panmujom is like a line-up between the heavenly world and the Satanic world. We must make a showdown in Korea. Korea's victory, particularly in the fight against Communism, is not Korea's alone.'

The Unification Church makes an all-out attack on Communism, and appeals to America to take a stronger stand against an atheistic ideology. In reply to questions whether he was linked to the South Korean government, or the C.I.A., Mr Moon retorted, 'that is absolute nonsense. Ours is a religious movement and we get no instructions from the government.'

Unusually for a religious movement, the Unification Church seems to have a good deal of money. In Korea the movement owns factories making machine tools and has been accused of manufacturing armaments. In reply it is said that the South Korean government obliged industries to assist in the production of weapons, and the Unification factories only produced parts, supplying five per cent of the requirements for M16 rifles. Mr Moon has obviously been a very successful business man, and he has lived in luxury, but the very brief summaries of his life that are available speak only of his youthful religious experiences, arrest and sufferings, and final formation of his church. There is hardly a word about his business activities and if they were honest they should not be hidden. The sale of Ging-seng tea from Korea is said to finance most of the work in Japan. Some of the members of the church have given all their goods to the church, and others work long hours selling pins and flowers. When asked why he did not allocate some of his money to feeding the hungry, Mr Moon replied, 'we are doing some welfare work', but other people are caring for the poor and orphans and his 'unique role' was to bring man to an awareness of God.

In a critical study of the Unification Church, based on years of research, Dr Eileen Barker of the London School of Economics, dismisses charges of brain-washing or holds that it is inefficient as only ten per cent of those who pass through Moonie workshops are converted to the movement, and even smaller numbers remain for more than two years. Moonie converts often come from respectable, happy and religious homes. They are moved by 'open-minded idealism', looking for an alternative to materialism and the rat race of western society. However, the high rate of lapse suggests that most find that they must look elsewhere.[1]

The Unification Church claims to be Christian, to teach the Fatherhood of God and love to neighbour, but with less emphasis upon Christ than upon the Founder. There are comparable movements, especially in America, which also idealize their founders, and they naturally arouse criticism from older established churches. Mr Moon is a Korean, and might have been less noticed as an American revivalist. He is also rich and finances expensive activities such as conferences in the best hotels, but this is in the pattern of American religion, and countless capitalists have spent great sums on social and religious organizations.

The Archbishop of Canterbury has said that 'the Unification Church is not a Christian organization and has nothing whatever to do with the ecumenical movement'. This may mean that it does not belong to the World Council of Churches and that its aim of unifying churches and religions has not been accepted.

Professor Frederick Sontag, a California philosopher, after visiting many centres of the Unification Church, left open the question whether Sun Myung Moon is 'conveying a message from God that still today is hidden beneath his overt doctrine'. Like other observers, Sontag seems to wonder what will happen if disillusionment sets in among the followers of Moon, will the last state be worse than the first? Or 'will God step in to restore destruction when the Moonies' human power fails or runs amuck?'

[1] *The Making of a Moonie,* 1984.

Chapter Fourteen

BORDERLINE RELIGIONS

Scientology Religion?

In 1967 an application was made to the Registrar General of the United Kingdom for a Chapel of Scientology to be registered as a place of religious worship. This would have exempted it from rates and allowed the celebration of marriage ceremonies. In 1963 a certificate had been refused to the Mormons, because their buildings were not open to the public.

The Registrar refused the Scientologists also, but on different grounds, arguing that their meetings were not religious worship. He had examined a book of *Ceremonies of the Founding Church of Scientology*, and declared that 'prayers were not used in the service', which 'need not be solemn and "reverent" '. He found no reference to a Creed or its being recited, and while there was a choir at services it was not stated 'what they sang'.

It seemed that the Registrar had not consulted professional theologians or liturgical experts, since some of his statements are questionable. The use of a Creed has not been an essential part of all Christian worship. In the early church it was a confession of faith at baptism, it did not appear in the regular Roman liturgy until the eleventh century, and was rejected by many Free Churches at the Reformation. The use of hymns is modern, not provided for in the traditional Anglican Book of Common Prayer, and even prayers are optional among Quakers.

In 1969 an appeal was brought against this judgement to the Queen's Bench Divisional Court in London and heard by three judges, including the Lord Chief Justice. They accepted a definition of 'worship' which had been used in the case of the Mormons, when Lord Evershed had said: 'I am content to take the relevant meaning given in the Shorter Oxford Dictionary, namely, "the actions or practices of displaying reverence or veneration to a being regarded as Divine by appropriate . . . rite or ceremonies." '

Known for having an interest in the definitions of religion I was sent a transcript of this appeal. Checking the reference to the Shorter Oxford English Dictionary it was found to be incomplete and seemed misleading! Worship was there defined as 'Reverence or veneration paid to a being or power regarded as supernatural or divine'. The dictionary definition was wide, and perhaps had Buddhism in mind in referring to 'a being or power', and 'supernatural or divine'.

At the appeal Justice Ashworth and his fellow judges used the incomplete definition, declaring that 'there is no profession in the creed of any belief in God or indeed in any deity', and refusing the Scientology application. It seems that their defending counsel, Mr Quintin Hogg (later Lord Hailsham) did not question the use of the definition. Similarly at a further appeal in 1970 Lord Denning declared, according to the transcript, that a place of religious worship connotes 'a place where people come together as a congregation or assembly to do reverence to God. It may not be the God which the Christians worship. It may be another God, or an unknown God, but it must be reverence to a deity.' He admitted that there may be exceptions, such as Buddhist temples, but 'apart from exceptional cases of that kind . . . it should be a place for the worship of God'. It is a large exception, since Buddhists number hundreds of millions, and the religion of the Jains though much less numerous also does not include the worship of a supreme God.

It seemed worth while to look at practice as well as literature and a visit was arranged to the Scientology headquarters at East Grinstead. This is an old building in extensive grounds, and there were class rooms with students at work. There were pictures of the founder, Ron Lafayette Hubbard, and texts suggested his pervading presence: 'Don't rush, you might run into Ron.' It seemed like 'Big Brother is watching you.' There was a chapel and a 'religious' service, at which the choir sang with the voice of dogmatism, 'this man alone, made the way known'. There was a minister with a clerical collar and a cross or ankh, leading hymns and a time of quiet or prayer, and a sermon which mentioned God several times. These may be religious trappings, but not necessarily its essence.

The Registrar and appeal judges seem to have concentrated upon the Sunday service, as described in booklets, though Justice Buckley did look at an account of a wedding ceremony. He commented, 'I can find nothing in the form of the ceremony set out which would not be appropriate to a purely civil and non-religious ceremony . . . It contains, I think, none of the . . . elements of worship.'

But a marriage ceremony is primarily a social contract, and other services may be more significant. Scientology services for christening or Naming of Children, and burial of the dead, are important, the most universal sacraments and rites of passage. Here it is clear that Scientology believes in a *thetan*, an immortal soul under a name derived from the eighth letter of the Greek alphabet and perhaps related to its symbolical oval shape. The service says that 'the main purpose of a Naming ceremony is to help get the thetan oriented. He has recently taken over his new body.' Similarly the Funeral Service helps the soul to a future life: 'Go now, dear (deceased) and live once more, in happier time and place'. These are spiritual beliefs, but the relation of human and divine needs further consideration.

Religious or Secular?
Lord Denning agreed that 'the adherents of this philosophy believe that man's spirit is everlasting and moves from one human frame to another: but still, so far as I can see, it is the spirit of man and not of God.' Admittedly God is not so dominant or

transcendent in Scientological doctrine or practice as in Christianity, Judaism or Islam. God is called the Eighth Dynamic, the highest level of reality which one attains when the Seventh Dynamic, the spiritual universe, is 'reached in its entirety'. A book of *Scientology Religion* has the aim 'to help the individual become aware of himself as an immortal Being . . . his relationship to others . . . and the Supreme Being.' *Customary Service* says that 'man's best evidence of God is the God that he finds within himself'.

Scientology, like some other modern movements, has been influenced by eastern religions, especially Buddhism. Reincarnation is a Hindu and Buddhist conviction. Belief in God also (perhaps with a small 'g') may be more akin to the neuter Brahman of India, really identical with the human soul or self, than to the transcendent God of Semitic religions. It is claimed that the goal is 'individual salvation in harmony with other life forms, the physical universe, and, ultimately the Supreme Being. It is in this Eastern tradition that we find the background of Scientology.'

If Scientology is compared with secular organizations the religious nature of its beliefs becomes apparent, even if its theology is not fully developed, and there may be signs of change of emphasis. It is quite different from political societies which are not interested in immortal souls. It is distinct from social clubs, like the Oddfellows or the Order of Anglo–Saxons. It is more akin to Freemasonry which has beliefs in a kind of God, the divine Architect, and in spiritual beings. Freemasons often say that their society is not a religion, though it has marks of religious belief and ritual. But there are reasons for this denial since in Europe, at least until recently, Freemasonry has been strongly anti-clerical and its membership forbidden to members of the Roman Catholic church. In Britain and the United States Freemasons have often been members of the churches and would not wish to claim their organization as a rival religion.

Scientology claims to be scientific, a comparable claim to that made from the last century by Christian 'Science'. It employs methods of physical and mental training, and its teachings and practices have attracted much criticism, either as unscientific, or as brain-washing, or as appropriation of goods, or as libelling its opponents. Its methods of mental training may be compared with other systems, such as Pelmanism, but differently from other organizations of this kind, Scientology seems to have adopted from the beginning a spiritual attitude to life as a basic doctrine.

The Founder and Aims of Scientology declare that their purpose is to free man from the bondage that 'sought to reduce him, to the status of cells, brain and body, a "scientific" lie which has caused untold damage to man and which, unless corrected will eventually result in total annihilation.' And again it is affirmed that 'man is primarily a spirit, immortal and basically indestructible'.

The outside observer will want to know whether the beliefs of Scientology are fulfilled in practice. Are its methods of physical and mental training well-founded, well-intentioned, healthy and helpful? What are the costs, and are they proportionate to the results? Are public and private activities proper and open? Scientology can claim to be a religion probably in the light of its teachings on the spiritual nature of human beings. It has also claimed to be a 'church', though that word seems to be derived from the Greek 'Lord's (house)' and traditionally has therefore been a particularly Christian title. But it is the moral and social practices that require attention, 'by their fruits you shall know them'.

Modern Witchcraft?

Having written a book on witchcraft in Africa and Europe I have been trying to live it down ever since. It was intended as a critical study, and meant to help people in Africa who may be accused of witchcraft or join in accusations against others, usually women, suspected of anti-social activities. But interest in witchcraft has brought invitations to many kinds of society in Europe, religious, social and political.

It is a strange feature of the vaguely religious atmosphere of our time that there has been a revival of belief in witchcraft, and it is practised—or so it is claimed. Abandoned by the educated from the seventeenth century, and wilting among the populace under the impact of scientific rationalism in the nineteenth, belief in witchcraft seems to have re-emerged in the West in the twentieth century. Along with it has come much else that may be described as occult or esoteric among the uneasy intelligentsia.

In Africa today as in the past there are almost universal beliefs in the presence and power of witches, and all manner of ills are attributed to them, from infant mortality to failure in examinations. There are traditional witch-doctors, who are not witches themselves but seek to doctor and heal those who are thought to have been bewitched. And there are modern anti-witchcraft societies, often run by young men who make money by claiming to find out witches in dances and ordeals.

The late Margaret Field, in *Search for Security*, made a classic anthropological and psychological study of African women who had been accused of witchcraft, and some of whom had confessed to impossible actions. The conclusion was that witchcraft was purely illusory. Countless people have been accused of it, but the fault is in the eye of the beholder. There are no witches, properly speaking. The witch-hunters have projected on to innocent people their own fears and fantasies; they have provided easy but false explanations of sudden death, jealousy between wives, failure of crops, sterility, accidents to lorries, lack of promotion in work, in fact any misfortune.

Of course there are some nasty old women, who may curse their neighbours in bad temper. And there are nasty old men who may prepare harmful potions, or stick thorns in images, but Africans have usually distinguished these sorcerers and workers of 'bad' magic, from the witches who are thought to fly by night and eat human souls or 'the soul of the flesh'.

There are many similarities between the witchcraft beliefs of modern Africa and those which were held in medieval and Renaissance Europe and which led to many witch-hunts and persecutions. There seems to be no evidence of one continent borrowing from another, but some of these ideas are very ancient and may have been widespread in prehistoric times.

Accusations of witchcraft made against European women seem to have been no more true than those which are made in Africa. People often confessed to the most impossible crimes, under torture or social pressure, but that did not prove the fact. The accounts of witchcraft and the supposed confessions were all written by the witch-hunters, Inquisitors and other agents, and they are usually worthless on matters of fact. Many people were executed, hanged in England and America, burnt alive on the Continent, but most of them were innocent of the crimes of which they were accused. Why then has there been a revival of belief in witchcraft, and how valid is it?

The Old Religions?

A five-yearly congress of the International Association for the History of Religions was being held in Rome. The delegates, who were accredited to this academic society from universities, were horrified to see a man join the British group dressed in dark robes and with a tall hat and claiming 'I am a witch'. One could almost hear French and German colleagues whispering, 'These English, not real scholars!' The British delegation disowned the gatecrasher and later made stricter rules for membership and for advertising its meetings.

This self-styled witch was Gerald Gardner who claimed to have a museum of witchcraft and a witches' coven at

Castletown in the remote and mysterious Isle of Man. The revival of witchcraft belief in Britain, and development of its practice, are often dated from the work of Gardner in the fifties and sixties.

From the Isle of Man Gerald Gardner sent out lucky charms and complex symbols, for a price, and he encouraged the formation of witchcraft societies. But since historical witchcraft in Europe was usually supposed to have been dangerous, Gardner and his followers professed to avoid harmful practices. Two major beliefs of both European and African witchcraft were that the accused people could fly through the air, and had communal meals at which they ate human flesh. These notions are reflected in popular pictures of witches on broomsticks, phallic symbols, and accusations of cannibalism which were common in the Middle Ages and in Africa, both of which suffered from widespread disease and high infant mortality.

Apparently modern so-called witches in Europe do not teach physical flying through the air, unaided by any machines, nor do they now claim to eat unbaptized babies as many of their predecessors were supposed to have done. To avoid suspicion of anti-social or impossible activities, Gardner and his followers made a distinction between Black and White Witchcraft. They were White Witches, of course, pretending to help people to develop supernatural powers, though perhaps they were not averse to uttering fearful threats and curses on those who might reveal their secrets.

Naturally, modern supposed White Witches do not agree with the critical analysis of Witchcraft as superstition and delusion. They often claim to be descendants of an Old Religion, the survivors of believers in a nature cult which existed in Europe before Christianity came along to spoil innocent fun. But such claims appear to be as spurious as the confessions. The records of medieval European witchcraft show no references to the true gods of ancient Europe: Woden or

173

Thor, or Dagda and Brig. People accused of witchcraft were said to have confessed to being followers of Beelzebub or Diana, Herodias or Lucifer, figures from Biblical and classical literature. The very names of the accused women in ancient records were Christian, the commonest being Elizabeth, Margaret, Mary and Alice. Medieval women were accused of making pacts with the Devil, celebrating a Black Mass, or listening to Satanic sermons, all of which were imagined perversions of Christian practice and not relics of a pre-Christian faith.

Research has been done into modern witches' meetings and has recorded claims that they worship the Life Force, or the powers of the sun and the universe. But such ideas owe more to the Life Force and the Elan Vital of Bernard Shaw and Henri Bergson than to ancient paganism or medieval witchcraft. As adepts become better informed they may be more careful to identify elements from pre-Christian religions with their own statements and practices, and a lot may be gathered from old and standard books, though it is not always accurately reproduced. But all this does not prove that witchcraft preserved ancient beliefs through the ages down to today, or that members of newly-founded societies are the legitimate followers of ancient religious cults.

It seems quite clear that there never did exist a witchcraft cult, and it lived only in the minds of the persecutors, such as the Inquisitor James Sprenger on the Continent, Matthew Hopkins in England, or Cotton Mather in America. Similarly there are no witches' societies in Africa today, only people wrongly accused of witchcraft. It appears also that there has been no continuous witchcraft cult, in Europe or Africa, and this 'ancient religion' has not been preserved till today.

There are indeed societies that claim to be 'covens', and there are also leaders who take pretentious titles like White Witch and Grand Wizard, but it is all artificial.

It may be claimed that witchcraft societies do no damage, and in a free country there must be room for a great variety of organizations some of which may teach absurd doctrines. There may be little harm in dressing up, gesticulating in magic circles and triangles, or dancing naked in the woods, as long as the public is not offended by obscenity or the dancers struck by pneumonia. But there may be dangers of threats or real injury to those who leave the society and divulge its secrets. Blackmail may be threatened against some who have been photographed in sexually suggestive postures. Like all secret societies, modern witchcraft groups are open to temptation and abuse, and to exploitation by mercenary or unscrupulous leaders.

Among the many religious movements of today organized witchcraft has limited appeal. It has no great scriptures or line of inspiring teachers, as have the historical religions. Yet belief in witchcraft and the occult is symptomatic of the religious uncertainty of our time, when people are a prey to innumerable physical and mental hazards, and their followers deserve a better faith than witchcraft leaders can give them.

Chapter Fifteen

AS OTHERS SEE US

Sad Christians

Travelling around among people of different religions brings illumination, not only of their various faiths but of Christianity itself. It is salutary to note some of the points that are made, some new, some debatable, some not apparently relevant. Many appreciations and criticisms have been made, and some are considered here.

'The best Christian in his most sublime moments is a sad man', comments Dr Kamel Hussein in notes to his historical novel on Good Friday, *City of Wrong*. This strange appraisal arises out of a discussion on why the disciples did not fight to defend Jesus when he was arrested, as the Muslims fought alongside Muhammad when he was attacked from Mecca. This brought a psychological stress, according to Dr Hussein, which has remained down Christian history.

From the events of Good Friday, he says, came 'that sadness which is a ruling element in the character of the greatest adherents of Christianity, their fear of sin, their love of self-reproach and abasement, their sense of the importance of the sin of Adam and their belief that it had to do with the anguish Christ underwent that mankind might be saved from its consequences. Perhaps all these hallmarks of Christianity are simply an echo of the great sin of the apostles' self-reproach, as if Christians are expiating this sin until the end of time.'

In his notes Dr Hussein remarks, no doubt rightly, that the first apostles had no idea of the later doctrines of Redemption or Atonement, of the divine significance of the Crucifixion, or that it had been ordained from all eternity. But he considers that such doctrines followed on from the self-reproach of the abandonment of Jesus.

It is necessary to distinguish the particular from the general statements. In the particular instance, whether the disciples should have fought to defend Jesus may be debated. If they had done so they would have acted contrary to his teaching on turning the other cheek, and it will be remembered that when one of them drew a sword and struck the servant of the high priest in the garden of Gethsemane Jesus rebuked him, according to Matthew, with the words, 'put up again your sword into its place; for all those that take the sword shall perish with the sword.'

Christianity became a religion of suffering, from the Crucifixion onwards through centuries of persecution, and there have been many martyrs during its history. By contrast Islam was a Success Religion, becoming known from France to China in the century following the Prophet's death. Though, as it was noted in an earlier chapter, Dr Hussein accepts that if Islam had suffered persecution in its early years God would have guided it through its troubles as Christianity was guided.

The more profound criticism is whether Christians have had an excessive preoccupation with the sense of sin, and the consequences of morbid self-reproach. Thus Dr Hussein says that 'Christians have inherited this rigorous sense of wrongness and sin. It has left on them an abiding impress, in the belief that every injury befalling any human soul is traceable to some sin he has committed.' This might apply even more to the Hindu and Buddhist beliefs in *karma*, and trouble resulting from some sin in present or past lives.

This is said to produce a negative morality. 'Faithful Christians are more eager to avoid wrongdoing than to promote good. Their fear of wrong is more powerful than their concern for justice ... In their exhortation they enjoin abstention from evil more than admonition to good. Thus negativism overcame all their actions in times when Christianity was most given to worship and piety.'

177

Christians may recognize such a picture as applicable to some saints in the past, or some other churches today. In discussions with Dr Hussein it seemed that he was thinking in particular of the Coptic Christians of Egypt, with their black-robed priests and monks living hard lives in desert cells. They have been a struggling minority for many centuries, and contrast with the large and public mosques and festivals of Islam.

Christians in western Europe and America may not recognize themselves as obsessed by sin and self-reproach. Perhaps our fathers did have such an obsession and it may have provided a stimulus to the 'Protestant work-ethic' as well as to the penitential systems of Catholicism. But many modern Christians may only have such a general sense of sin as was indicated by Calvin Coolidge who being asked what had been said by a clergyman who preached about sin, remarked, 'he said he was against it.'

Christianity was a Hebrew faith, in origin, which was interpreted and developed in Greek terms, and these two elements have complicated its intellectual and moral history. From St Paul, and particularly from the later Augustine, there developed the notion of the flesh lusting against the spirit, so that 'to be carnally minded is death, but to be spiritually minded is life and peace.' The development of the doctrine of Original Sin taught that 'all men are conceived and born in sin', which the Hebrew tradition had not taught. Applied to sexual morality this produced ascetic teachings which honoured virginity above the married state and, in the Roman Catholic church, imposed celibacy upon all clergy, monks and nuns. Even more than Buddhism, which allows priests but not monks to marry, Christianity emphasized the dangers of the flesh, putting together 'the world, the flesh, and the devil'.

Yet by a strange reversal of its traditional asceticism, Christianity is often now seen by the rest of the world as immoral. It condemns the traditional polygamy of Islam, Africa or China, yet its film stars are divorced many times and Henry

VIII stands as a grim example. In Asia and Africa pornographic books and films are imported from the West, with men and women professing shock but flocking to read and see them. The West is often regarded as both Christian and promiscuous. There is envy at its material progress, but also scorn and fear at its possession of nuclear weapons. It may be that Kamel Hussein's judgements of the Christian preoccupation with sin have been overtaken by events, or that in a nuclear age a sense of sin might be a needful corrective to the arrogance that holds the life of humanity in the hands of one or two heads of state.

Imperial Arrogance

The impact of Europe and America upon Asia and Africa has been profound and traumatic. Physical aggression went alongside more peaceful penetration: British and French shelling and bombing in northern Africa, the suppression of the 'mutiny' in India, the opium war in China, the list is endless. The establishment of colonial empires was eventually followed by their political dismemberment but often by remaining economic subservience, colonization by 'Coca–cola–nization'.

Alongside physical conquest went intellectual arrogance. The white races looked down on the rest of mankind as dirty, uncouth, and uncivilized. This was in strange contrast to the traditions of the people themselves. They had memories of past greatness, when there were cultures far superior to the West: in Egypt, Mesopotamia, Persia, India, China, Japan and other lands. But many westerners knew or cared nothing about this, for it was past and in a technological age irrelevant.

Then came further troubles. W. Cantwell Smith, a Canadian expert on the Islamic world, writes in *Islam in Modern History* of the feeling of betrayal by those Arabs who had adopted western ways. They had been told in effect, 'Give up those antiquated ways, those superstitions, those inhibitions; be modern with us, be prosperous, sophisticated. Emancipate your women, your societies, yourselves!' But when they did so, if a crisis arose in

179

political life they found that the West did not care for its converts. The feeling of betrayal was especially strong in the war in Palestine and the establishment of the state of Israel.

What is all this to do with Christianity? The separation of religion from politics, of sacred from secular, which has been attempted in the West is a concept very difficult for the rest of the world to comprehend. Islam has always fused religion and society, and in different ways so have India, China and the rest. So that western imperialism has been seen as of a piece with missionary imperialism, western morality as Christian morality, despite modern reversions of traditional Christian asceticism.

Cantwell Smith says that 'the bitterness of Arab disillusionment has gone very, very deep. It is illustrated in a charge that at 'Aka (Acre) during the fighting in 1948 the Red Cross—symbol and summit, as it were, of Western liberal humanitarianism or modern Christian goodwill—discriminated in its succour in favour of Jews against Muslims. Not only on the battlefield but in the hospital ward, the Arabs saw themselves repudiated as of no account.' Whether the charge was justified or not, it was revealing of Arab feelings.

In another example, some Egyptian writers have argued that the Crusades are still on, the struggle between East and West is the struggle between Islam and Christianity. One writer goes so far as to use the term Crusader for Christian, and Crusaderdom for Christendom and the modern West. The spread of secularism in the Islamic world is attributed to the machinations of imperialists and missionaries, to spread the notion that Islam is a religion of the past.

There is a rejection of the claimed moral superiority of the West. After wars they won, right supposedly conquering might, there was an assumption of moral leadership of the world. Partly this derives from Christianity but partly from national pride, and even our allies reject it when they speak of 'perfidious Albion'. That our word is our bond, honest dealing our custom, is rejected by those who feel themselves cheated and betrayed. They see us in more critical light, and judge our professions by our actions.

Again it is not all the social works of the churches, or the lives of saintly individuals, that attract criticism but general attitudes in which moral principles and racial attitudes have been mingled. But the religion itself, as well as morality, may come under fire.

Sapience

Belief in the superiority of the religion is one of the most powerful motives for missionary enterprise and it has taken men and women to the farthest bounds of the world. Preached by people with a higher social standing than the 'natives', there was often a response to appeals to abandon antiquated ways and emancipate societies. Christianity may have seemed superior because its agents were more successful than agents of other religions.

Missionaries taught converts to throw away or burn their idols, discard all wives but the oldest, cover up their nakedness, often adopt European clothes and live in model villages. Both the new religion and the morality were superior to those of 'heathen' lands, and this has often been accepted, with modifications. But now come reactions, and others sometimes see us now as inferior morally and especially spiritually to the 'mystic East'.

In 1981 Seyyed Hossein Nasr delivered the Gifford Lectures in the university of Edinburgh, the first Muslim and 'in fact the first oriental' to do so. His subject was *Knowledge and the Sacred* and the aim of his long and detailed discussions was to justify the 'sapiential tradition' of the East, seen as 'the source of light', against the desacralization and rationalism of the West.

Dr Nasr is a well known and highly educated Muslim from Iran and formerly chancellor of a technological university in

Tehran, where he had entertained me and where the Shah's aim of making Iran the Japan of the Middle East was attempted. But Dr Nasr is also deeply versed in Islamic mysticism and in Indian philosophy, and the two are brought together in his first sentence which affirms that 'in the beginning Reality was at once being, knowledge, and bliss,' terms from the Hindu tradition which are said to be among the names of Allah in Islam.

It is not easy to define the 'sapience' of which Dr Nasr writes at such length. It is called 'the sapiential dimension' and the 'way of knowledge and sapience', or 'esoteric and sapiential knowledge'. On the one hand it seeks to restore the mystical way of seeking reality, against 'the desacralization of knowledge' in rationalism, and on the other hand it elevates the pantheistic or monistic philosophy of a major Hindu school of thinkers. Hinduism is considered to be 'the oldest of religions', though Judaism or Zoroastrianism may have as good a claim. The 'master of Hindu gnosis' is the monistic philosopher Shankara who championed the identification of human and divine in his exposition of the Upanishadic phrase 'you are That'.

Dr Nasr is concerned about the secularization not only of the West, but of the East also. For its sacred traditions have been undermined by 'historicism, evolutionism, scientism, and the many other ways whereby the sacred is reduced to the profane.' Even those western scholars who have sought to interpret oriental religions and philosophy have, with a few exceptions, helped towards 'the secularization of the East'.

The rationalism and secularism are traced through nineteenth century evolutionists back to the French philosopher Descartes of the seventeenth century, and ultimately to the ancient Greek philosophers with their rational studies. Christianity comes in for attack because in modern studies of the Bible, a 'so-called higher criticism' has destroyed or veiled 'the sapiential dimension'. For the religious or mystical traditions modern Christianity has substituted a purely ethical message and has forgotten 'the way of knowledge and sapience'.

It is strange that some writers on mysticism, including Dr Nasr, tend to regard it almost as the possession of the Orient, 'the source of light', and neglect or dismiss the long and widespread mystical traditions and saints of Christianity, in both eastern and western churches, and from the Bible onwards. For Dr Nasr Christian mysticism has 'become nearly completely emptied of intellectual and metaphysical content.' This is a highly debatable assertion, which could be countered with many examples from Christian mystics. For him, however, the only way for the West to revive its mystical knowledge of the Sacred is by 'authentic contact with the Oriental traditions'.

Dr Nasr is right to criticize the rationalism which blinds people to the profound apprehensions of religion and philosophy, but the cure is not necessarily the monistic philosophy of India. If the Orient is 'the source of light', and all the great historical religions arose in Asia, yet they do not all teach the same, and although Dr Nasr claims that there is 'but one Tradition', yet the religions are notoriously different in their expressions, for example Islam as against Buddhism, or Zoroastrianism against Shinto.

Christianity, like other religions, has had many failings. Its highly developed organizations may have developed from Roman imperialism, its acceptance of scientific method may not always be applicable to the devotional life. But the way forward may not be acceptance of the pantheistic views of Hinduism or seeking a vague orientalism. Dr Nasr in himself seemed to combine western-style education with Islamic mysticism, and those of us who have long studied many religions may seek to combine the best in East and West, the mystical and the critical.

183

Church and Christ

Do others see us only as imperialists or racialists, obsessed with sin or lost to the mystical dimension? Has Christianity, with twice the membership of the next largest religion, no respected status among the faiths of the world?

Christianity is indeed respected as a world power, leading figures like the Pope are honoured when they teach peace and reconciliation, and social works are appreciated by ordinary people. But curiously, for those who maintain that religion and society are one, distinctions are made between the church and Christ. The Gospels are studied the world over, although they were written and preserved and translated by the church.

Christ is revered as a prophet in Islam, an Avatar in Hinduism, and a Buddha or Bodhisattva to some Buddhists. The teachings and healings of Jesus, his love and compassion for the outcast, evoke universal admiration. The doctrines that the church wove around him may be rejected or misunderstood, but there is no doubt of the appeal of his personality to many people of different religions. In fact, the modern 'critical' study of the Gospels, so decried by Dr Nasr, has succeeded in uncovering the human Jesus from the veils of dogma and the frozen attitudes of stained glass windows which had hidden him for centuries. It is probable that there is greater knowledge and appreciation of the human Jesus now than at any time since the first Christian generation.

But Christ is almost separated from the church, in the non-Christian mind, or the church is considered only to be praised in so far as it draws near to its divine exemplar. Rabindranath Tagore, the great modern Indian poet, wrote to an intending Christian missionary: 'Your Western mind is too much obsessed with the idea of conquest and possession; your inveterate habit of proselytism is another form of it. Christ never preached himself or any dogma or doctrine; he preached love of God. The object of a Christian should be to be like Christ—never like

184

a coolie recruiter trying to bring coolies to his master's tea garden.'

The pride of race, sect, or personal superiority, is condemned—by the example of Christ. The missionary notion of sacrifice might be a form of self-indulgence. 'Preaching your doctrine is no sacrifice at all—it is indulging in a luxury far more dangerous than all the luxuries of material living. It breeds an illusion in your mind that you are doing your duty—that you are wiser and better than your fellow-beings.' So, and perhaps this was what Hossein Nasr was seeking, the goodness of Christ is held up to Christians. Tagore continued, 'On the spiritual plane you cannot *do* good until you *are* good. You cannot preach the Christianity of the Christian sect until you be like Christ—and then you do not preach Christianity, but love of God, which Christ did.'[1]

In the same spirit Mahatma Gandhi distinguished between Christianity, or Christian practices, and Christ. 'It is a great pity', he wrote once, 'that Christianity should be mixed up with foreign dress and foreign ways of eating and drinking.' And to missionaries he said that 'if they could have refrained from "telling" India about Christ, and had merely lived the life enjoined upon them by the Sermon on the Mount, India, instead of suspecting them, would have appreciated their living in the midst of her children, and would have directly profited by their presence.'

The positive element in the way others see us is that they look beyond us to Christ. 'Merely' to live the life of the Sermon on the Mount has always been an ideal, with struggles to approximate to it. But to make Christ and his ideals clear is still a task, for how 'they' see him may be as distorted as how we have seen him.

---

[1] C. F. Andrews, *Mahatma Gandhi's Ideas*, 1929, pp. 356–9.

How they see Him

Christ has been regarded as an Avatar by Hindus, one of the succession of ten or more which includes both mythical and historical figures. In an earlier chapter twelve characteristics of Avatar doctrine were distinguished, some of which may be paralleled in the doctrines of Christ and others which differ, especially that of repeated Avatars or incarnations.

Some Hindus and theosophists have seen resemblances between the stories of Krishna and Christ, so that borrowings or even a common original have been suggested. The very names Krishna and Christ have been compared. But Krishna is a Sanskrit name meaing 'black' or 'dark', the god of dark-skinned people, whereas Christ is a Greek word for 'anointed', translating the Hebrew title Messiah, 'the anointed one' of God.

In popular Indian story the baby Krishna's life was threatened by a king, but with divine help he was taken away to another country and given to cowherds among whom he grew up. The angry king massacred all the children but young Krishna grew up working miracles and defeating demons. But superficial resemblances disappear before the many differences and the story taken in context. The wicked king Kansa was cousin to Krishna's mother Devaki and had been warned that one of her sons would kill him. He had six of her children put to death, but the seventh and eighth were incarnations of Vishnu, Balarama and Krishna, and they were preserved miraculously. Kansa was always sending demons to destroy Krishna but in the end Krishna not only killed him but brought back his six murdered brothers from the infernal regions and took them up to heaven. After many adventures, with 16,000 wives and countless children, having reigned in triumph Krishna died by being shot in mistake for a deer by a hunter with the appropriate name of Jaras, 'old age'.

More plausible parallels have been drawn between the infancy stories of Jesus and those related about the Buddha, and as these developed around the beginning of the Christian era the Buddhist might have influenced the Christian, or vice versa. The Buddha was born miraculously and a sage predicted his future, later he was tempted by a demon, he worked miracles, chose disciples, and foretold the end of the world.

Some of these statements are general and might be related about many religious leaders. As far as Buddhism goes a scholar has remarked that 'in proportion to the investigator's direct knowledge of the Buddhist sources' the number of parallels seems to decrease, from nine, to five, to one.

In popular legend the Buddha made a resolution eons ago to become a Buddha and after many births was reborn in the lowest heaven, whence he descended to earth. His parents were married, a king and queen of the warrior caste, and in a dream his mother saw a white elephant entering her womb, which was interpreted as the conception of a son who would either become a universal monarch or a Buddha. The child was born under a tree, caught by four gods in a golden net, and the infant at once took seven steps and proclaimed in a lionlike voice, 'I am the chief in the world.'

The closest comparison to the infancy of Jesus has been seen in the story of Asita, 'the Buddhist Simeon', but this parallel may also fade away if looked at in detail. Asita was a sage who lived in the Himalaya mountains and heard the gods rejoicing in the birth of the Buddha. He flew through the air to the palace of the Buddha's father and repeated the prophecy that the child would either become a universal monarch or a Buddha. The sage wept that he would not live to see this and after receiving presents he flew back home. But the Bible story of Simeon, in Luke's Gospel, is quite different and Hebrew. Simeon was a just man who lived in Jerusalem and was brought by the Spirit into the temple when the parents of Jesus took him there to present him to the Lord. Simeon had been told by the Holy Spirit that he would not die before he had seen the Christ, and he took him in

187

his arms, blessing God that now he could die in peace, 'Lord, now lettest thou thy servant depart in peace, according to thy word: for mine eyes have seen thy salvation.'

In the Islamic world Jesus is seen in the light of the Koran, born of a virgin by the word of God, teaching and working miracles, not crucified but ascending into heaven, and perhaps to come again to kill the Anti-Christ. In apparently denying the Crucifixion the Koran stated of Jesus that 'they did not kill him and did not crucify him, but he was counterfeited for them' or 'only a likeness of that was shown to them.' This seems to mean that they thought they crucified him but were mistaken. In an earlier chapter the suggestion of a substitute being crucified for Jesus was rejected, and Kamel Hussein quoted as saying that 'no cultured Muslim believes in this nowadays.' However there are some who do believe this.

In the sixteenth century a so-called Gospel of Barnabas was compiled by an Italian monk named Marino who became converted to Islam. His 'Gospel' contained the story of Jesus based on the canonical Gospels but, unlike them, with Judas taking the place of Jesus on the cross. This work is some three times the length of Matthew or Luke, and it contains long discourses and repetitive rhetoric as well as a reworking of the life of Jesus, but the chief point is the substitution at the cross.

The Koran said that God raised Jesus to himself (4, 156), and 'Barnabas' asserts that when God saw 'the danger of his servant' he commanded the archangel Gabriel to 'take Jesus out of the world' and he was removed from the upper room by a window and placed 'in the third heaven in the company of angels blessing God for evermore'. Then Judas impetuously entered into the chamber, whereupon God acted wonderfully so that 'Judas was changed in speech and face to be like Jesus.' Judas was arrested, tried and crucified, protesting his innocence, and crying at the end, 'God, why hast thou forsaken me, seeing the malefactor has escaped and I die unjustly.'[2]

This Gospel of Barnabas seems to have been unknown to the Muslim world until there was a passing reference to it by the first English translator of the Koran, George Sale in 1734. An English translation of it was not published till 1907, but it has been used since then in some Muslim polemic. At a Christian-Muslim dialogue in Tripoli in 1975 the delegates were provided with copies of the Koran and the Gospel of Barnabas. When the Vatican participants protested the latter was withdrawn, but no Bibles were forthcoming. In 1979 the Muslim Information Services in London issued a book entitled *Jesus, A Prophet of Islam*, claiming that the Gospel of Barnabas was 'the only known surviving Gospel written by a disciple of Jesus', and maintaining that it had been accepted as canonical until A.D. 325. Others claimed that it was 'the only Gospel which preached pure and unmixed monotheism', but after early circulation 'it remained in oblivion for about 1500 years until it was discovered in the eighteenth century.'

A different line has been taken by the Ahmadiyya sect, the followers of the Indian Ghulam Ahmad (died 1908). Although varying from orthodox Islam, this movement has done much propaganda, especially in Africa. Again the crux is the denial of the death of Jesus. The Ahmadiyya hold that Jesus was crucified but he was taken down alive from the cross and recovered. He then travelled about the east, arrived in Kashmir in northern India and died as any other man in old age. This contradicts the orthodox and Koranic teaching that God raised Jesus to himself, and this phrase is translated in a popular Ahmadiyya English version of the Koran as 'Allah exalted him in his presence.'

The reason for the Ahmadiyya claim that Jesus died in Kashmir is not only that their movement arose in India but that

<hr>

[2] D. Sox, *The Gospel of Barnabas*, 1984.

in Srinagar there was said to have been a tomb of a Muslim prophet called Yus Asaf. It was perhaps originally a Hindu tomb, but then taken as Muslim, and the name Yus is said to be the same as the Arabic name for Jesus which is Isa. Although it is claimed that 'hundreds of thousands' of men, and ancient documents, affirm that the tomb is that of Jesus Christ, critical scholars have found no such testimony, either oral or written. There are countless tombs in India, and innumerable holy men, and the claims have been thoroughly sifted and rejected.[3]

Orthodox Islam maintains that Jesus did not die, and only minorities vary the explanations. Here is one of the major differences between Islam and Christianity, and the latter can only continue to provide the evidence given in the four Gospels. As with comparisons with the stories of Krishna and Buddha, the Christian witness is in the Bible.

[3] H. J. Fisher, *Ahmadiyyah*, 1963, p. 70f.

Chapter Sixteen

IS THERE A MISSION?

The Heathen

On our first Sunday in Japan, at a mixed English–Japanese university chapel service, the congregation sang Bishop Heber's verse:

> What though the spicy breezes
> Blow soft o'er Ceylon's isle
> Where every prospect pleases
> And only man is vile,
> In vain with lavish kindness
> The gifts of God are strown,
> The heathen in his blindness
> Bows down to wood and stone.

When Heber wrote that hymn in the early nineteenth century he had not left England and knew little or nothing of Ceylon (Sri Lanka). In the first version he wrote 'Java's isle', but somebody must have told him that Java was strongly Muslim and its people would be even more shocked than Christians at the thought of bowing to idols. The line was changed to Ceylon, though it did not scan, but the Ceylonese were mostly Buddhists who would also have repudiated bowing to wood and stone. The many images of Buddhism represent supernatural beings and they, not the idols, are the objects of devotion. It is now generally recognized that even other 'heathens' do not worship material objects, any more than Christians worship crosses or images of saints.

It is pleasant to note that when Heber travelled round India, as second Anglican bishop of Calcutta from 1823 till his death in 1826, he came to 'think highly . . . of the natural disposition of the Hindoo'. He wrote in his journal composed for his wife of 'kind-hearted, industrious, sober and peaceable . . . a manly and courageous people'. This was different from other missionaries who in public reports, to gain support for their work from home, tried to depict Hindus and people of other faiths as utterly depraved because of their evil religion. Charles Grant, an ardent evangelical, wrote of 'the immorality, the injustice and the cruelty of Hinduism', and its adherents 'as depraved as they are blind, and as wretched as they are depraved'.

The hymn in Japan was taken from a local compilation called *The English Hymnal*, of 300 standard hymns in English with facing Japanese translations. In the congregation native English speakers sang the English version, while Japanese sang their own parallel hymn, somewhat discordantly in effect. It was said that the Japanese version of Heber's hymn was less pointed than the English and did not give a corresponding term to 'heathen', yet the impact was similar, in condemnation of worshippers in other religions. Listening to Japanese sermons, with interpretation, it could occasionally be remarked that Buddhism and Shinto provided easy illustrations for some belief or custom that the Christian preacher was opposing. But then, such may be heard in the West where preachers sometimes condemn the idolatry or even another religion by name, in the absence of believers in that religion who have no chance to answer back. The absent are always wrong.

The word 'heathen' meant originally a dweller on the 'heath', the wild country areas when Christianity was spreading through the towns. The old religion was more persistent in the country, and a 'pagan' was a 'peasant', a rustic country labourer in the same sense. Both these words are quite inappropriate for followers of the great religions of the world, at least, and should no longer be used, in fact they have often been replaced. One reason for surprise at the hymn sung in Japan was that the verse quoted has disappeared from some modern hymnbooks in the

West and it was alarming to find it still in use in Japan with its large Buddhist and Shinto population. Likewise phrases like 'o'er heathen lands afar', have been changed in some modern hymnals to 'o'er lands both near and far', and Kipling's Recessional which spoke of 'heathen heart that puts her trust', has been dropped.

Telescopic Philanthropy

Christianity has always been a missionary religion, with a message to all races. The teachings of Jesus, given in Aramaic, were written in Greek in the Gospels and the whole New Testament was put out in this international language for the Gentile churches. Christianity was occasionally and severely persecuted for three centuries, but it continued to spread, was legalized by Constantine and soon became the official religion of the Roman empire. Priests and monks went far and wide, in and beyond the empire, and notable in missions were the Nestorians who, although they preferred to speak of Mary as Mother of Christ instead of Mother of God, were otherwise orthodox and took churches and schools right across Asia. When Marco Polo visited China in the thirteenth century he noted that there were Nestorian churches in many towns, and some of their monuments remain to this day.

With European explorations and trade from the fifteenth century Roman Catholic missions went to both Asia and the Americas. Protestant missions received a great impetus from the Evangelical Revival of the eighteenth century, and within ten years of the death of John Wesley in 1791 five of the chief British missionary societies were founded. In 1799 a 'Mission connected with the Evangelical part of the Church of England' was founded which soon became known as the Church Missionary Society for Africa and the East. It was decided that Sierra Leone should be the first scene of work, for a settlement had been founded there for liberated African slaves in 1787 and it became a British Crown Colony in 1808. It was hoped that the freed slaves would assist in the evangelization of their own lands, and protection would be afforded by the British Crown.

This and other expeditions were attacked by Dickens in *Bleak House* (1852) as 'telescopic Philanthropy'. One of their home workers, Mrs Jellyby, had 'handsome eyes, though they had a curious habit of seeming to look a long way off', while her house was in disorder. Mrs Jellyby's daughter, Caddy, declared 'I wish Africa was dead . . . I hate and detest it. It's a beast.' There were many other critics of Victorian missions, often like Dickens on the grounds that money and workers were being sent overseas while men, women and children were ground into drudgery and poverty by factories and industries in Britain. Disraeli in *Sybil* and Cobbett in *Rural Rides*, were but two of those who joined in appeals to divert attention to needs nearer home. Nevertheless the missions continued and in the 'white man's grave' of West Africa many young men and women died of fevers within a few weeks or months of arrival.

Samuel Ajayi Crowther, mentioned in an earlier chapter, was one of the freed slaves sent from Sierra Leone back to Nigeria as a missionary, and being accustomed to the climate he had a long and active life. Crowther was included in the first expedition to what is now Nigeria, before he became a bishop, because of his 'trustworthiness and steadiness as a man of established Christian character'. He wrote journals of this and later expeditions which were published and acquired immediate fame, giving details of social and religious life.

Dickens mocked the proposed settlement on the Niger as Borrioboola-Gha. Its name is Lokoja and it is now a small town near the confluence of the rivers Niger and Benue, but it did not develop as had been hoped. Crowther co-operated with a Manchester cotton merchant, Thomas Clegg, and with T. F. Buxton who had founded an African Native Agency Committee to provide funds for cotton gins and instructors in cotton cultivation and carpentry. The aim was to form self-sufficient communities to spread, as Livingstone said elsewhere, Christianity and Commerce.

Such plans for industrial and agricultural work were criticized in England, but the secretary of the missionary society quoted St Paul making tents as well as preaching, and Crowther declared that 'missionaries must instruct in horticulture as well as Christianity'. There were heavy casualties among the missionaries, however, although later expeditions fared better by using quinine, though the malarial mosquito had not yet been identified as the cause of the fevers.

In 1861 there were attacks by the local population on the mission in the Niger Delta and the mission secretary, Henry Venn, went to the Admiralty and persuaded the government to send out three steamers and a gunboat. Two villages on the Niger were destroyed for attacking a British ship, and a second gunboat took Crowther up to Lokoja. He asked the mission to ensure that he had passages and after his consecration he went up the Niger again on a gunboat, confirming, preaching, founding churches and schools, and encouraging trade and agriculture.

In the following years there were fewer gunboats, but money continued to come out from England to Crowther. He became virtual British consul on the Niger, sending and receiving gifts to local rulers, from the Niger Delta to the Muslim emirates of the interior. He was the best known visitor in these regions and is recognized by modern critical historians as the most powerful influence at that time on the Muslim rulers.

Missionary Religions
This example has been given because of personal knowledge of Lokoja and its history, but also as one illustration of the methods of some Christian missions in modern times. But Christianity is only one of the world's missionary religions, and in assessing the

value or otherwise of missions other religions must be taken into account.

There have been three major missionary religions, which in historical order are Buddhism, Christianity and Islam. Other religions were more ethnic or national, such as Hinduism or Shinto. It used to be said that to be a Hindu one had to be born into a caste and believe the Vedic scriptures. The latter would be easier than the former, at least in this life. Yet there were Hindus in Bali and other non-Indian parts of southern Asia, and missionary Hindus today try to convert non-caste tribes in the jungles and hills of India. Then the modern Hindu missions, the Ramakrishna Missions, Hare Krishna, Divine Light, and other organizations try to win recruits from the religions of Europe and America.

Shinto, the Way of the Gods in Japan, required recognition of the emperor as descended from the Sun Goddess, and most Japanese still believe this in spite of the Human Declaration in which the emperor announced that he was in no way 'divine'. In the Shinto revival of the eighteenth and nineteenth centuries, during which Buddhism which had been in Japan over a thousand years was denounced as a foreign religion, there was an apparent extension of Shinto. The Japanese empire then spread over Korea, Manchuria, Taiwan and much of China, and later into south-east Asia. This was to be the 'co-prosperity' rule, with Shinto and Japanese rulers on top, but there was no real mission to convert other peoples or to allow them equality in a Shinto church.

Buddhism, which arose in India in the sixth and fifth centuries B.C. cut across caste and national barriers, especially in its monastic orders but also among the laity. The Buddhist emperor Ashoka in the third century B.C. is said to have sent his son and daughter as missionaries to Ceylon and other monks and nuns to south-east Asia. Later Buddhist missionaries went to Tibet and China and eventually reached Korea and Japan.

Indian ideas were thus taken right across eastern Asia, but they also went to the north and west. According to Clement of Alexandria in the third century A.D. monks had come as far as Egypt teaching 'the precepts of Boutta'. In our day Buddhist teachings and missionaries have flourished in Europe and America, in a new burst of fervour stimulated in doubt by Christian missions to Asia, returning the compliment by sending their missions to us. California has been claimed as a new centre of the Buddhist Dispersion.

Islam expanded the most rapidly of the missionary religions, spreading from Arabia to France in the hundred years after the death of Muhammad. After days of skirmishing with the troops of Charles Martel the Arabs folded 'their tents' and 'silently' stole away. In modern military jargon it would be said that their lines of communication were overstretched, but Muslims remained in the south of France and Spain for centuries. Along with the armies there were Islamic preachers who consolidated the religious gains. That they were not always immediately successful is shown by a statement that the Berbers of north Africa apostasized twelve times before remaining Muslims. Islamic empires dominated the Mediterranean for centuries, ruled the Near and Middle East and India, and the faith extended to China where it still has some twenty million adherents. Islam has remained a missionary faith, and in modern times it has developed in lands round the Indian Ocean and spread from north Africa into the tropical regions. With immigration to western Europe there have come many Muslims, over a million in Britain, replacing the Jews as the largest non-Christian religious minority.

Christianity has already been referred to, with its missions past and present, and it has become the most widespread of all religions, with followers in nearly every country in the world. But in modern times a new missionary faith has appeared, in Marxist or Leninist Communism. Whether Communism is a religion has been debated. It has some of the marks of a religion: a faith in inevitable progress, in invincible Communism, in 'an objective law independent of man's will', in the inevitable triumph of revolution. There are Marxist sacred and infallible texts, great state parades like old imperial processions, banners and enthusiasm. Marxist eschatology, the doctrine of the 'last things', the coming perfect state, owes much to Jewish and Christian hopes for the Kingdom of God though it is only on earth.

The success and wide diffusion of Communist ideals have a religious air, the major difference from the older religions is in the rejection of the supernatural or spiritual, God and the human soul. Religions claim that their message is more than human and this-worldly, it is inspired by God or the eternal truth taught by Buddhas. Even for the most sympathetic Communist the extrahuman origins of religion remain unproved, though he might admire religious efforts to surpass the sufferings of the human condition.

Nevertheless in considering whether a missionary religion can be justified, account must also be taken of the unceasing missionary efforts of Communism. The urge to convert other people to our ideals remains strong, and Communism is as dogmatic as other religions, claiming that it alone has the ultimate truth.

Scriptures
The possession of scriptures or remembered teachings of their founders gave missionary religions advantages. African traditional religion had no writings, priests and people being illiterate. Therefore it also had no written history and no religious autobiographies. It was largely tribal and limited in outlook. Islam and Christianity came with the advantages of being international, historical and scriptural, and they profited from these assets as well as from political and commercial imperialism.

It was much the same in other places where illiterate religious beliefs gave way before scriptural missions, among hill and forest tribes in India who today are being converted to Hinduism. In south-east Asia Buddhism came to dominate the illiterate peoples, but it also had to face the literate.

When two literate religions faced each other conversion was not easy. Buddhism and Jainism both rejected the sacred texts of Hinduism, even when they were not written down but passed on orally by priests, since their own doctrines were regarded as superior. After success lasting over a thousand years Buddhism went down in India before resurgent Hinduism and militant Islam. Elsewhere Buddhism adapted itself in syncretistic manner to Taoism in China and to Shinto in Japan.

Buddhism translated its scriptures into many languages, but there is room for much research into the extent of this translation work. Certainly innumerable Buddhist texts were translated into Tibetan, Chinese, Japanese, and many languages of south and east Asia. The amount of Buddhist missionary translations is incalculable, but the fact should perhaps act as a warning against claims that the Bible is the most translated book, for that would be difficult to prove conclusively.

Islam published its scriptures, but in Arabic, not in translation until recently. The Arabic language has been one of the world's greatest international tongues and it stimulated the writing of other languages. This fact has often been underestimated in the West. In the article on Herbert Spencer in the *Dictionary of National Biography* it is astonishing to read a statement that his *First Principles* had been 'translated into all the chief languages of the world and into many minor languages such as Arabic and Mohawk'! This, of one of the few truly international languages, which has made the scriptures of Islam known in Arabic over tens of thousands of miles. The printing of the Koran has developed even more in modern times and a press in Saudi Arabia claims to print seven million copies each year.

Translation of Communist texts is a great industry and publication is widespread from Russian, Chinese and many other centres.

Christianity is unusual in several ways. It is unique in accepting the basic scriptures of the parent faith into its own canon of holy writ, making an *Old* Testament parallel to a *New*. Although Islam recognized that there were other 'Peoples of the Book', that the Torah had truly been revealed by God to Moses, and the Injil or Gospel to Jesus, yet the Arabic Koran that came to Muhammad has always been regarded as true and if copies of Torah or Gospel differ from it they must be distorted or wrong. Christians have accepted the revelations given in the Old Testament, though the New Testament is a fulfilment of the Old, the New Covenant which replaces it.

The Christian Gospel was written in Greek, not the language of its Founder, and it has been translated into many languages. The sales of the Bible from Christian publishing houses has passed five hundred million in a year, with the complete Bible in over 270 languages and the New Testament in many more.

To missionaries, ministers and catechists credit must be given for the vast amount of literary and translation work they undertook. They reduced languages to writing and produced the Bible as the first piece of literature in many tongues. Samuel Crowther, for example, compiled grammars and dictionaries of Yoruba, Igbo, and Hausa, and translated parts of the Bible into those languages.

A further remarkable fact is the part that some Christian missionaries played in translating scriptures of Asian religions into European languages. This was no doubt for the use of their own workers, but in so doing they helped the cause of the comparative study of religion. The famous Baptist missionary William Carey translated the Bible into Indian languages, such as Bengali and Mahratta, and compiled grammars and dictionaries. But he also edited in three volumes the great Hindu heroic and religious epic, the Ramayana, the story of the incarnate god Rama (1810). In Ceylon the Wesleyan missionary Daniel Gogerly translated some of the Buddhist Suttas from Pali (1846). The Rev J. M. Rodwell translated the Koran in 1861. While the Analects of Confucius were translated by Italian and French priests, and by Protestants James Legge (1861) and W. E. Soothill (1910).

With such firsthand acquaintance made available to the West through missionaries and other scholars, the teachings of Asian scriptural religions were bound to produce a new situation for Christian missions. Translations, studies of theology and philosophy, accounts of rituals and customs, pictures of imagery and architecture, and discussions with religious teachers, all combined to present much better accounts of the religions of other peoples than had been possible on such a scale in previous centuries. The religions of Asia had been in closer contact with each other, Buddhists with Taoists and Shintoists, and even Hindus and Muslims sometimes appreciated each other's mystical intuitions. But European Christianity had been virtually isolated, until the easy communications of modern times opened up new worlds of thought and faith.

Dogmatisms Meet
There have been, and still are, some Christian missionaries who regard all non-Christian religion as the work of the Devil. The Cables and Gladys Aylward in China spoke about the Devil in other religions, and fundamentalist missionaries in many lands still speak in this way. If they do not openly denounce idolatry as devil-worship, they assume that other ways are wrong and their way is the only one to salvation, better indeed than that of other Christians, especially those who have been toying with 'heathen philosophy'.

On the positive side there are supremacist and exclusivist statements to be found in Christian scriptures and history. Every speaker on comparative religion is used to being questioned on the verse attributed to Christ by the writer of the Fourth Gospel: 'I am the way, the truth, and the life. No one comes to the Father but by me.' This may be interpreted of the universal Christ, through whom all other ways may pass, or of a special knowledge of the Father which need not exclude other understandings of God. But there are other statements in the scriptures of the supremacy of Christ, and indeed such faith seems to be part and parcel of devotion.

Comparable attitudes are found in other religions. The Bhagavad Gita seeks to reconcile different ways of faith but it always asserts the supremacy of Krishna: 'whatever form a devotee seeks to worship, it is I that ordain it' (7, 21), and 'I am the origin of the whole world, and nothing higher than me exists' (7, 6). In Milinda's Questions the Buddha is the supreme, the most distinguished, without an equal and matchless. In many other places the Buddha is called the exalted One, unsurpassed as a guide to mortals, the teacher of gods and men. In Islamic devotion the Prophet may be called he who traversed the seven spheres, the spreading dawn, the light of lights, the intercessor for all creatures.

It is natural for devotion to bestow the highest titles on its adored object, but should these be made into dogmatic statements and used not only to affirm but to exclude? And in the light of the knowledge of other religions, which were virtually unknown in the past, is not re-interpretation of apparently exclusive texts needed? Indeed apologists are well aware of the danger of quoting isolated texts, because there are others that suggest different attitudes. Paul's preaching at Athens, referring to an unknown God and quoting Greek poetry, was one of the first attempts to make a link between Christian faith and another. In the Fourth Gospel itself there are verses that suggest a wider view than that quoted above. In a comment on this Gospel Archbishop Temple quoted the verse, 'the light that lighteth every man', and he wrote, 'By the word of God—that is to say by Jesus Christ—Isaiah and Plato, Zoroaster, Buddha and Confucius, uttered and wrote such truths as they declared. There is only one Divine Light, and every man in his own measure is enlightened by it.' In a similar spirit more recent church pronouncements have been made to recognize the truths, and the salvation, to be found in different religions.

Some modifications of the traditional denunciation of other religions can be seen in both individual and official statements. The Second Vatican Council issued a major *Declaration on the Relation of the Church to Non-Christian Religions*, which stated that 'the Catholic Church rejects nothing which is true and holy in these religions'. Some faiths were singled out for their special contributions: 'Thus in Hinduism, men probe the mystery of God and express it with a rich fund of myths and a penetrating philosophy.' In Buddhism men and women are taught how 'they can achieve a state of complete liberation, or reach the highest level of illumination'. Then 'the Church also regards with esteem the Muslims who worship the one, subsistent, merciful and almighty God', who 'venerate Jesus as a prophet', and 'pay honour to his virgin mother Mary'.

The Declaration may appear to be guarded, but it seems to have been the first time that a church council pronounced in this way. And in introducing the decree to the Council Cardinal Bea touched on the question of the salvation of people in other religions: 'they can be saved if they obey the command of their conscience . . . who live according to the command of their right conscience.' Therefore it was 'the very grave duty of the Church to enter in every possible way into a dialogue . . . to lead them into a full and explicit participation' in the riches of faith.

This was a far cry from the assertion of Bishop Cyprian in A.D. 251 that there is 'no salvation outside the church'. This was directed against heretical baptism, but it was often taken later to mean that there was no salvation outside the Church of Rome. In modern times, however, such rigid dogmatism has been modified, and in 1952 Father Feeney and a group of Catholics in Boston who maintained the rigid view were rebuked by the Holy Office, which declared that 'a person who stated that no one out of the Church could be saved was himself out of the Church and excommunicated.'[1]

A conclusion drawn by some theologians is—'that man is never saved through any religious system. Only God can save man through the influence of his saving grace. . . . Does God use the religious traditions of the non-Christian world in the fulfilment of his will of salvation, which extends to all people? If he does so, or at least may do so, these religions are a providential means of salvation for their adherents'.[2]

If theologians recognize that other religions can be providential means of salvation, then it may be asked whether there remains any need for a mission. Usually in the past, and among fundamentalists today, it has been assumed that all those who were outside a particular and limited scheme of salvation were lost, doomed to burn 'in living flame', as Cortes said. But if this view of a restricted salvation, and its corollary of eternal damnation for the rest of mankind, are rejected, as they are by many Christians today, then does any place remain for a mission?

The words of Rabbi Isidore Epstein in his book on *Judaism* may be relevant: 'Judaism was a missionary religion', when it was confronted by the paganism of the Graeco-Roman world. 'But when paganism gave place to Christianity and later also to Islam, Judaism withdrew from the missionary field and was satisfied to leave the task of spreading the religion of humanity to her daughter faiths.' For while these two religions were

[1] J. Neuner, *Christian Revelation and World Religions*, 1967, p. 33.
[2] ibid. p. 13.

'lacking the true vision of the one and only God', they shared many religious and moral truths with the mother faith.[3]

Might it be said that Christian missions should be similarly restricted? Certainly not addressed to Jews, probably not to Muslims, perhaps not to Buddhists and theistic Hindus, and efforts reserved for idolaters and illiterates. The modern concentration of missionary effort upon Africa, with its great success, might suggest that mission planners, consciously or unconsciously, have directed their efforts to places where there were fewer scriptures or rival teachings. The lack of Christian missionary success among the scriptural religions, Islamic, Buddhist and Shinto, may have provided further reasons for directing attention especially to Africa.

But it seems unlikely that any of the three great missionary religions, Buddhism, Christianity and Islam, would publicly abandon their long-held international aims. And today they are joined or rivalled by other missionary faiths. Hindu teachers have broken out of restriction to India and have become Gurus to Europe and America. Communism has world aims, it is influential over half of mankind and seeks to convert the other half. In face of this rival alone it would be strange for ancient international religions to abandon their mission and it is clear that Islam, for example, has no intention for doing so.

The mission may remain, but the methods used may change. There are different methods to be used in imperial and post-imperial countries, and in scriptural and illiterate cultures. The approval that is often given to medical missions, but withheld from propagandist work, indicates a deep feeling that the faith is to be expressed by service and that a little help is worth more than sterile debate.

Two sentences from *Christian Revelation and World Religions*, indicate the way in which thoughtful missionaries have come to

[3] *Judaism*, 1959, p. 144.

view their task in the light of the knowledge of other living religions:

'1. It is important to disown any conception of the mission that means conquest, and to embrace the idea of a humble offering of God's saving truth and love to free human beings.'

'5. Service should always be rendered in a spirit of dialogue in which either party is ready, before speaking, to listen to God in himself and in the other, so that both may fulfil the redemptive plan of the love offered to mankind.'[4]

[4] J. Neuner, *op.cit.*, pp. 22–23.

Chapter Seventeen

TEACHING RELIGIONS

Australian Nerves

The religions of Asia and Africa are known in many parts of the western world today, by their literature, teachers, communities and temples. Teaching is also given about such religions in many schools, though not without some opposition. Some twenty years ago the minister for education in New South Wales proposed that the syllabus for education should include teaching on other religions than Christianity. There was an immediate outcry from some Australian church leaders. They demanded to know why heathen religions should be taught to their children, was not Christianity taught well enough, and did not that suffice? Ministers of religion had the right of entry into schools, but were they expected to teach rival religions to their own, or countenance their propagation?

I was in Australia on a lecture tour and was interviewed by the press at Sydney university. After general matters the question was raised about the row over inter-religious education. I protested that the details were not clear, there was no right to comment, and a visitor should not interfere. The reporter persisted: were the churches making too much fuss, did they reveal their own ignorance about Asian faiths, did British churches object to such teaching? I was prodded into remarking that such teaching had been given in Britain for many years, it took place in church schools as in others, so perhaps the Australian churches were unduly nervous.

Next day the *Sydney Morning Herald* carried a banner headline, 'World Authority Thinks Churches Unduly Nervous'. I kept that 'world authority' to impress the family, but protested to the reporter that a casual remark had been made into a formal statement, and there was no mention of reluctance to comment on a local issue on which details were not clear. It looked like misrepresentation and it would have been better to keep to the rule of saying nothing to the press, but he replied that there would be a different headline next day and people would forget it.

Australia seems to be well placed to study Asian religions but little was done until recently. Perth is nearer to Jakarta than to Sydney, and the whole continent is much closer to China, Japan and India than to Europe. Australia's restrictive immigration laws have been breached to allow in some professional workers from Asian lands. There are possibilities of inter-religious dialogue, but little has been undertaken, and even aboriginal religion has received little sympathy except from anthropologists. Attitudes seem to vary between the desire of some clergy to destroy aboriginal religion, and the wish of conservationists to preserve it as a museum piece.

Australian art has become known abroad, and Australian literature, but it seemed that much of Australian Christianity was stuck in the past and made little effort to grapple with the problems of the twentieth century. The diocese of Sydney has been notoriously conservative, and gave little support to a lecture tour on comparative religion, which seemed to be regarded as a frightening subject. Things were better in Western Australia at that time where Archbishop George Appleton was noted for his sympathetic approach to Asian religions, particularly to those of Buddhist lands where he had spent many years.

Australian universities seemed almost as hesitant as the churches, hardly able to break through their traditional distrust of the study of religion as an academic subject. There were appointments in oriental languages and history but, until recently, little on religion. Now some new posts have been created for general religious studies, though there have been difficulties over applicants and appointments.

Teaching Religion

Whether religion should be taught at all in schools is viewed in different ways in various countries. In some lands, especially where there is a state church, religious instruction may be compulsory, though the manner in which it is done varies greatly. In other places there is an attempt at complete separation of the state from religion, and education is often regarded as secular. Yet there may be a teaching of 'morals', which often seems to be simple patriotism, a kind of substitute-religion. The ubiquitous presence of the flag in American schools and public buildings strikes many outsiders as a sort of totem pole, denoting faith in the American Way of Life as a religious ideal. Since schools in the United States are forbidden to teach religion, it might be thought that it would decline. Yet America has a higher ratio of churchgoers than many European countries, especially Britain and Scandinavia, which have state churches and compulsory religious education. It might seem that the less education there is about religion the more churchgoing prospers.

The use of prayers has been banned in American schools and the teaching of religion formally forbidden, though it is not possible to exclude all reference to it. Some schools and colleges have courses in world cultures, in which religions are important elements. Even Christianity may find its way in, as a major force in western culture, and religion is so pervasive that it appears in many contexts, such as history, sociology, art and music.

In specifically theological training there are curious situations. It seems almost incredible, yet it is true, that most colleges for teaching the clergy in Europe and America have no courses in the study of religions other than their own. Indeed there was probably more in the past, when there were returned missionaries who could give accounts of Asian religions, however negatively. But today, with few exceptions, clergy colleges concentrate on biblical, doctrinal and historical studies,

209

and neglect the knowledge of the religions of most of mankind. Yet there is great interest in the comparative study of religions among the laity, and the clergyman may find himself quite unable to provide guidance on problems that bother his congregation, such as yoga, reincarnation, or Zen.

It is often thought that there is a decline in the studies of religion in the universities of Europe and America, yet the opposite may be the case. The chief decline is in the number of candidates for ordination, which in some countries affects churches from Roman Catholicism to the Salvation Army. There are fewer ordinands, perhaps partly because of the many modern social services which attract men who might formerly have thought of the ordained ministry and work within the church. Further, women still cannot be ordained in some large churches, yet in most religions women form the majority of supporters.

In more general education there is greater and wider interest, and decline in numbers of ordinands does not imply decline in numbers of students learning about religion in broader senses. Many university students read about religion without the intention of ordination, perhaps thinking of doing social services or teaching, and large numbers of them are women.

The Universities Central Council for Admissions (UCCA) in Britain has published figures which show that there have been increases in students of religion in most years during the last two decades. These figures relate to those who study theology, or religious studies, as a first or second degree subject. There are many others who include religion as an option, which may be useful later in teaching. Moreover these figures refer to universities, and there are many other colleges which may include references to religion in some way among their studies. The great variety of religious studies, hitherto largely unsuspected, was revealed by the following example.

A report on the Governance of the University of London singled out the need for reorganization of studies of religion and theology, which seemed to be restricted to three colleges which were partly or wholly denominational. A committee was appointed to investigate and it discovered, to its surprise, that religion was already studied in many other places in the university. The School of Oriental and African Studies had a number of degree programmes which involved religious elements, with texts from religious scriptures in language courses and the study of religion in chosen areas of Asia and Africa. In this and other colleges there were courses in anthropology, sociology, history, geography, classics, literature, language, art and music, all of which might have some religious interest. There were plans to develop academic studies of religion; for example, in Judaism, Islam, archaeology, East European, Germanic, Scandinavian, African and Latin American studies.

An appended table to the report showed that in London University alone there were studies in Christianity in seven different degree syllabuses, Buddhism in five, Hinduism in three, Judaism in seven, and Islam in eighteen. While comparative religion, and moral and ritual systems, were studied in ten different ways. Add to this the studies undertaken in the forty other universities of the United Kingdom, and in many more colleges of education and polytechnics, and the startling fact emerges that religion is far from being the neglected backwater that is sometimes imagined. It plays a major part in many courses at the highest level. Hundreds of theses are being prepared in religious subjects in colleges across the country. The same could probably be said of many universities and colleges throughout the world, quite apart from specific theological or confessional studies, since religion is such an ancient and constant element in human life.

Teaching and Teaching about Christianity
The Shap Working Party on World Religions in Education was established in 1969 and took its name from a preliminary conference held at Shap in the Lake District of Britain. For eighteen years this voluntary and part-time organization of lecturers and teachers has organized conferences and published books and aids for teachers about the religions of the world. With this and other agencies at work, the teaching of world religions has become as well equipped as any subject in recent years. There is more possibility of factual and impartial teaching about the religions of the world than was formerly available, and the next generation ought to be better informed than the present. A great deal has been done to link up with immigrant communities and learn about their religion by visits and discussions. The tragedy hitherto has been that there have been relatively few qualified teachers of religious studies, and not enough schools allow adequate time for religious teaching.

The early Shap publications contained excellent annotated booklists on twenty major religions, from African to Mithraic, but there was no section on Christianity, and this great gap was only filled in the third edition of the Shap *Handbook*.

The reasons for the early omission of Christianity were certainly not anti-Christian prejudice, since several members of the Working Party were ordained ministers of different churches. One major factor was probably that Christianity, or Biblical knowledge, was already taught in most schools because British law decreed that an 'agreed syllabus' of Bible education must be provided. This is often neglected today, the law being ignored, or teaching given only in the primary classes, since some teachers are unable or unwilling to teach the Bible.

In other schools such teaching was done badly. In one school the children were taught the Old Testament one term, New Testament the next, back to the Old, on to the New, and so on for four years, by which time teachers and pupils were exhausted. Children had learnt lists of the kings of Israel and Judah, the life of Jesus, and the geography of Paul's journeys, four times and were tired of them, inoculated against Christianity for life.

When years have been spent in primary and lower secondary classes on teaching about Christianity, supposedly covered in elementary Bible lessons, it is natural to look farther afield in the higher classes. Religions of immigrants and new communities can be studied, their meeting-places visited, and broader principles of religion can be considered with reference to other faiths. Here the many aids to teaching that are now available provide needed guidance.

But there are problems in the teaching of Christianity. The teaching methods that may be applied to other religions, critical and impartial study from the outside, have often been hardly tried on one's own faith. Some teachers have wanted to criticize, and others have sought to convert, and whether either attitude is appropriate for a school has been debated.

Moreover, Christianity, like Islam and Buddhism, but unlike traditional Judaism and Hinduism, is a missionary religion. It has therefore had complex and sometimes conflicting attitudes towards other religions, and the teacher may either condemn all the others, or suggest an accommodation with them.

Further, as a world religion, and by now far the most extensive, Christianity is not just European or American but also Asian and African. Its very extent and complexity make it difficult to study. There are enormous differences between, say, the Maronites of Lebanon and the Southern Baptists of Georgia. Which Christianity does one teach? Further still, there are emotional problems in teaching about one's own religion in school, or even in criticizing the religion of one's own culture.

The teacher of religion, at any level, is liable to some heart-searching, and if it were not so it might suggest that he did not really believe in the importance of his subject. In studying

Christianity, or any religion, sympathy with the subject is essential. Committed faith need not be a hindrance, provided it does not seek to influence the children unfairly, but conviction of the importance of the role of religion in human life is invaluable.

A Christian teacher, or for that matter a Buddhist or an agnostic, may be asked to keep his convictions out of the classroom, but is that desirable or even possible? If the pupil is to gain some convictions, should not the teacher also have some? Otherwise he may give a merely superficial knowledge of his subject.

In secular state schools the attempt to avoid any religion, or to indicate a neutral position, may result in giving the impression of an anti-religious view of life, which becomes the agnostic orthodoxy of the school. Then the committed religious teacher may be unable to express his views and the conclusion may be drawn that they do not matter. In face of varied religious or anti-religious attitudes students may ask questions: 'Which is right? What do you think? Do you believe in God?' If nothing is said, then neutrality leads to indifference. A teacher who has religious or moral principles may express them in other subjects, but if he is forbidden to mention them in specifically religious teaching then the whole enterprise may be undermined.

These are some of the problems that face teachers of religions today, and there are no easy answers. When other religions are studied there are further problems, and it is essential to show fairness and sympathy even towards beliefs that we do not share. Pupils need to be led to make their own decisions, but they will not make them if decisions are regarded as unimportant and no guidance is offered.

The teacher may show himself also to be engaged in the search for truth and decision-making. If he has embarked on teaching about other religions he teaches facts 'about' them, but he may go deeper and look for the perennial questions which underlie all religions. Then he may 'teach religion', as essential to life though different in forms, engaging not only intellect but heart and will. In his own religious development the teacher is doubly fortunate. He can continue his search in his daily work, and be paid for doing it.

Chapter Eighteen

SEEKING AND SHARING

Dialogue

When the Assembly of the World Council of Churches met at Nairobi in 1975 some observers were invited, among them a Jew, a Muslim, a Sikh, a Hindu and a Buddhist. The invitations aroused controversy, and while the leadership was anxious to welcome the visitors, some delegates ignored them and others clearly wished they had not come. Some representatives wanted a condemnation by the Assembly of the Israeli occupation of Jerusalem, and others insisted that 'Jesus was not really of the Jews', or that nobody had the right to speak about Jesus who did not accept him as a personal Saviour.

The observers were impressed with the talking power of the Assembly. One remarked, 'I believe I heard five hundred Christian sermons in three weeks. But something was left out too. There were only a few hours given to study of the Bible, and none to any other text.'

On general affairs it was remarked that 'no trendy issue was left unvoted (racism, sexism, et al.) but none was much illumined by historical or revelational light.' Further, Christendom 'remains firmly clerical'. Not only Orthodox and Anglicans, but other American and West European churches were chiefly represented by bishops and pastors. A Jew wondered whether the church of Jesus, a lay man of the people, 'who had harsh words for clerical pomp', had been 'delivered into the hands of a Sadducean hierarchy'.

These are harsh words too, though they may show how others see us. But perhaps the Assembly, which is a business conference of world churches, was not the best place for interreligious dialogue. In the end it was a Norwegian archbishop who opposed dialogue on such occasions, and it seems unlikely that open invitations to World Council of Churches assemblies will be given again, or that if they are it will make much impact on inter-faith relations.

The World Council of Churches has a proper department for Dialogue with People of Living Faiths, and it has engaged in contact with leaders of other religions. Similarly the Roman Catholic church has given active encouragement to inter-faith dialogue and has expressed this in formal statements, like the *Declaration* from the Second Vatican Council which was quoted in the last chapter but one.

Such movements are new on the part of the whole church, though there have been many contacts between individual members of the religions in the past. It is important that official recognition should now be given to some of the elements in other faiths which can be approved from within a different religion. It is important to note the common elements, distinguish families of religions, and indicate the essential differences and particular characteristics of a faith.

Many conferences have been held between representatives of different religions: Jews, Christians and Muslims; Hindus and Sikhs; Buddhists and Jains; and any or all of them in other combinations. Doctrines have been explained and attitudes towards social and economic concerns. Sometimes it is complained that each representative of a religion tends to repeat his own entrenched position, so that there may be little meeting of minds and even less of devotion, and the best of conferences needs to be followed up by practical exercises in which ordinary believers can share.

There have been joint retreats, for practice of meditation and yogic exercises. Common celebrations have been held, for example, of Christmas or the birthday of Muhammad, since nobody doubts that he and Christ were born. Passover and Easter have obvious links, though the manner in which they are celebrated, as in other inter-faith worship, goes beyond historical remembrance into prayer and praise, and this gives rise to complications.

Inter-Faith Worship

A service for the British Commonwealth was held at the church of St Martin-in-the-Fields, London, at which Her Majesty the Queen was present. The participants, naturally in a multi-racial and multi-religious Commonwealth, represented different religions and a programme was drawn up to include readings from the scriptures of Christian, Jewish, Muslim, Hindu, Sikh and Buddhist faiths.

After this service some religious newspapers printed protests against a church being used for such a mingling of religions, with the use of non-Christian texts, and under pressure from the diocesan bishop this famous church was closed to inter-faith services. Later celebrations of this worship were held in secular buildings like the Guildhall, in college chapels, and finally found their home in Westminster Abbey. The Abbey is a 'royal peculiar', not under a bishop but with a Dean who is appointed by the Crown. The recent Dean is President of the World Congress of Faiths, and many leading members of Asian religions, such as the Dalai Lama, have been welcomed at Westminster Abbey. The London Society of Jews and Christians has its annual garden party in the ancient Abbey gardens.

The closing of a church to inter-faith worship illustrates some of the problems of religious co-operation. Similar services have been held in other churches, synagogues, and mosques, with varying success. It has been easier in some Free Churches and Liberal Synagogues, and more difficult in High or Low churches or Orthodox synagogues. There has been much debate on the advisability of such joint worship and whether it is really helpful to members of the religions involved.

In inter-faith worship there may be losses as well as gains, and there is a danger of seeking the lowest common denominator. This may result in anything distinctive of a particular religion being left out, and Christian beliefs are susceptible to such pruning. Christian prayers generally, as shown by the collects in prayer books, have normally been addressed to God the Father through our Lord Jesus Christ. In inter-faith services, however, Christian prayer to God may be used but reference to Christ omitted, and to Christians this may suggest a diminution of faith.

Only last year at an All Faiths Service, there were readings from Buddhist scriptures which praised the Buddha and recounted his stories in devout terms, recitation of passages from the Bhagavad-Gita in which Krishna is hailed as supreme God, and verses from the Koran emphasizing belief in one God. But the representative of Christianity chose a passage from the epistle to the Romans and openly stated that 'Jesus is not mentioned'. If there is a religion without Jesus does it remain Christianity?

The same problem is found in Bishop Kenneth Cragg's anthology of Muslim and Christian prayers, *Alive to God*. This is a brave and imaginative attempt at providing understanding and communion between these two sister religions, but vital elements of Christian prayer are omitted in the absence of devotion to Christ. And Muslim devotion probably suffers in some way, if not to the same degree, since there is no mention of the mediation of the beloved prophet Muhammad. The missionary Constance Padwick, whose *Muslim Devotions* was quoted in an earlier chapter, states of the role of Muhammad in prayers that 'every detail of the human figure is treasured and loved, as well as the details of the mystical and super-human figure built over it.'[1]

[1] p. 146.

If distinctive elements are removed the religion loses much of its dynamic, and this may weaken inter-faith worship, which instead of joining devotions may become indifferentist. Does this mean that we cannot pray with our brother Muslims or Sikhs? Surely not, though silent prayer may be better than emasculated coalition-worship.

To the ordinary lay person worship in church or mosque may look much alike, but to point out the differences may bring a deeper understanding of the faith as much as by singling out common elements. A deaconess of the church of Scotland was charged with the care of immigrant women in a Scottish city. She got to know a group of Pakistani Muslim women so well that one day they suggested she might lead their prayers. She remarked, 'I can say with you, there is no god but God. But I cannot continue the testimony that Muhammad is the apostle of God, in the sense in which you mean he is the last and greatest prophet.'

They were surprised, because they had not realized there was this theological difference between the religions. For them, Christians ate pork and drank alcohol, which are forbidden to Muslims, but arguments about articles of belief were beyond these lay people. They had heard of Jesus as an Islamic prophet, but had not heard of the debate about his actual Crucifixion.

For the lay person, and for the informed leader, it may be more helpful to practise inter-faith worship in the full context of another particular religion. Churches and synagogues, mosques and temples, are usually open to visitors of any faith or none, but they proceed with their own worship without abating its doctrine or practices. To observe the procession of the Scrolls of the Law, or to hear the chanting of the Adi Granth, may give more religious understanding of Jews and Sikhs than to read selected and abbreviated verses from their scriptures in a general anthology.

Sharing

Not only and perhaps not chiefly in shared worship, but in mutual respect, understanding and study, members of the different religions of the world can learn from one another. In a materialistic and often antagonistic world those who believe in a spiritual universe are drawn together.

Many Christians have been reluctant to get into contact with members of other faiths through fear of syncretism, the mixture of ideas and practices which it is thought would corrupt and change the faith. The foreign air of Japanese churches perhaps comes partly from memories of persecutions of the past and the desire to be different from the traditional culture. In our Tokyo college chapel there were no flower decorations, though Japanese *ikebana,* flower arrangement, is world famous and could be adapted to church usage, so 'foreigners' thought.

There have been, however, notable Japanese supporters of a more understanding approach to other religions and customs. During the imposition of the emperor–cult, before and in the Second World War, the president of the International Christian University in Tokyo, Kyozo Yuasa, refused to bow to pictures of the emperor as manifest God, and was persecuted for it. But afterwards, shortly before he died, Kyozo Yuasa declared that Christians needed to co-operate more with Buddhism and Shinto and that Christianity should be adapted to Japanese culture.

Professor Doi of the Christian Center for the Study of Japanese Religions in Kyoto has suggested four ways in which Christianity could develop in his country. First, following the example of Buddhism, it could accept the traditional respect for the dead. Then it should develop a theology of nature, on the lines of Shinto. Next it should work out Christian symbolism based on traditional culture, which would include architecture and church decoration. Finally, and perhaps most important, as Buddhism became a religion for the masses by a radical

221

simplification of doctrines, so Christianity needs to develop away from the teachings of a small minority of intellectuals and make radical simplifications in order to become indigenous.[2]

The well known novelist Shusaku Endo, a born Roman Catholic, has pleaded for a Japanese Christianity distinct from the customs of the West: 'the Japanese must absorb Christianity without the support of a Christian tradition or history or legacy or sensibility'. He goes on to plead for a religion which can express 'the full symphony of humanity', though for him 'only Catholicism can present the full symphony. And unless there is in that symphony a part that corresponds to Japan's mud swamp, it cannot be a true religion. What exactly this part is— that is what I want to find out.'[3]

Endo's thesis has been applied by some of his readers to religion beyond Japan. In the early centuries Christian doctrine was interpreted in Hellenistic terms, but if this does not fit Japan there are many who consider that it no longer fits the West either. In recent years there have been many debates about the understanding of the nature of Christ for today, how to interpret the 'myth' of the Incarnation. Most of such discussions only look at the western environment, but there are two other major factors which are ignored at our peril.

The first is that Christianity is no longer the property of Europe and northern America. There are greater numbers emerging in Africa and Latin America, with important minorities in India, the Philippines and other Asian countries. In reinterpretations of Christian doctrine these countries are equally important with the older strongholds, and many of them have a closer acquaintance with other religions.

The second factor is in the contact today of Christianity with other religions, about which all this book has been concerned.

[2] *Search for Meaning through Inter-faith Dialogue*, 1976.
[3] *Silence*, 1978, p. 14f.

The Christian faith must be rethought for the East as well as for the West, and it may learn from traditions that formerly were regarded as hostile or that were simply ignored. What does the Incarnation mean for today? Can Jesus be understood just as an Avatar, one of many? He was a man, and his humanity is probably better understood now than in many past centuries. But was he a prophet, like others? If he was the Christ, what does that mean to modern Christians, west and east? What is the meaning of the title Son of God, for modern men and women? If Christians say that 'God became man', do they really mean Son of God, and how important is the doctrine of the Trinity?

These and similar questions require other books or even a library for full consideration, but now they need to be placed in the context of the whole world. We can learn by sharing with the Hindu belief in the omnipresence of God which may affect statements about God 'entering' the world at the Incarnation. From Hindus and Buddhists may be learnt the value of meditation, and the discipline of body and mind in yoga exercises, and this can help prayer life. In Islam and Sikhism God may be seen speaking to men after the Bible and outside the Judeo-Christian tradition, showing in a wider sense than the epistle to the Hebrews that God has revealed himself 'at sundry times and in divers manners'.

Had God So Willed
The Prophet Muhammad was puzzled and disturbed by the divisions among the People of the Book. The Jews criticized the Christians, and the Christians disagreed among themselves. Both communities rejected the claims of Muhammad to be a true prophet, after the Bible, so that he cried, 'O People of the Book, why do you dispute?'.

This comes as a refrain many times in the early chapters of the Koran and at last the Prophet accepts that the divisions seem to be a mystery of the divine will. All that we can do is to rival one

223

another in good works, and at the resurrection God will declare to us the truth behind our differences.

The full verse reads: 'Had God so willed, he would have made you one community. But he has not done so, in order that he might prove you in regard to what has come to you. So strive to be foremost in good works. You will all return to God, and then he will tell you about the things in which you have differed' (5, 53).

It is a brave statement, tolerant of religious differences in a way that has been lacking in some other religions. But others have also said that 'by their fruits you shall know them', and that to do the will of God and care for the least of his creatures is more important than simply to cry 'Lord, Lord'.

Some recent writers have distinguished three attitudes towards other religions: Exclusive, Inclusive, and Pluralist. The Exclusive maintains that only its own teaching is right and all other ways are excluded. The Inclusive seeks to bring other teachings within the range of its own faith. The Pluralist recognizes that there are different ways, which may run parallel to each other.

The Pluralist position is not satisfactory if it is taken to mean that religions will forever run parallel to each other without any mutual effect, for one great feature of today is that all religions may be affected by others. In the past there were common themes in the Semitic tradition, between Christians, Jews and Muslims, and in the Indian tradition or the Chinese. But now ideas of God or life after death, or practices of devotion and meditation, may go from one major tradition to another.

The Pluralist position is also unsatisfactory if it is taken to mean that all religions are the same, which they are clearly not, or that it does not matter what people believe. Questions of truth and goodness are important. The religion of the ancient Aztecs, who held up the beating hearts of their victims to the sun, was clearly not so good a faith as the peaceful way of the Buddha.

A particular version of the Inclusive position seems to be that of Fr Raymond Panikkar who has written of *The Unknown Christ of Hinduism*. He maintains that whatever good there may be in Hinduism must come from God, and many men and women have found faith and salvation in this tradition. Yet, Panikkar holds, there is still a Christian mission to Hinduism. Christ needs to be made known there, the historical Jesus and his teachings, the crucified and risen Lord. This is the *Known Christ*, though the mission and the manner in which he is proclaimed need to be adapted in places and methods.

And is it True?
In his poem 'Christmas' John Betjeman put the Christian claim in dogmatic terms, raising the level of the question with which this book began:

> And is it true?   And is it true,
>   This most tremendous tale of all . . .
> That God was Man in Palestine
> And lives today in Bread and Wine.

The ardent faith is admirable and this poem is often quoted at Christmas, but from within Christian theology itself, let alone from the viewpoints of other religions, its terms may be questioned. That 'God was Man' is not a Biblical expression, for the scriptures state more carefully that 'the Word was made flesh'. That God lives in bread and wine may imply a doctrine of transubstantiation, limiting it to the presence of God or the risen Christ in the Eucharist. The Biblical teaching is much wider, 'I am with you always', and 'abide in me and I in you'.

Betjeman puts his claim against the 'tissued fripperies' of Christmas decorations and presents, and says rightly that none of these 'can with this single Truth compare' of the Incarnation. It is an uncompromising declaration of faith, and it may be compared with dogmatic claims made by the devout in other religions.

A believer must have an assured faith of his own, this is true to me, because God speaks to me here. But problems arise if we go on from affirmation of our own faith to negation of the faith of others. Must they be converted to precisely my expression of belief in order to obtain salvation or a full life? Muhammad was no less dogmatic than Betjeman, but he saw the wisdom of leaving the diversity of religion to God, who would reward men according to their works at the resurrection. Their communities would have been different 'had God so willed'.

In the modern world there is far more communication between all kinds of religion than in the past. We are pilgrims on what several religions call 'the Way'. Seeking and sharing, with an inherited faith of one's own, or simply a point of view, there may be still more light to break through from the words of God to people in different cultures.

It is often asked whether study of other religions weakens one's own faith. It may be maintained, on the contrary, that faith can be strengthened by finding new understanding and practice beyond our own cultural traditions. As Greek language and concepts helped to develop the Hebrew elements in early Christianity, so the wisdom of the Indian and far eastern traditions may enlighten our modern understanding. There may be a two-way traffic, of Christian views to the East and of eastern to the West. Then the more diverse understandings of God and man that are available today may lead to a revival of religious thought. A knowledge of Indian wisdom may help in interpreting our own expressions of doctrine, and may also help Indian churches to be more fully rooted in their own culture.

A new kind of mission may develop by both learning and sharing. There are Christian ashrams, retreat centres, in India, which seek to express Christian faith in Indian garb. The Benedictine monk Bede Griffiths has a church in the style of an

Indian temple, coloured and decorated with sculptures in Indian fashion. Indian robes are worn by the priest and church members, Hindu 'caste' marks are applied to the body in worship, with actions taken from Indian tradition. Some of the externals are adopted from India, yet this is a Christian monastery with a Christian liturgy. Bede Griffiths declares that the emphasis upon sacred history and liturgy comes from Judaism, Christianity and Islam, but it is brought into expression through Hindu concepts and practices. We must be true to our own tradition, he says, but open to all that others can tell us of the spiritual life.

Some modern missionaries have made the most experiments in dialogue and sharing, and at times their own communities are more conservative. Having been taught in the past to reject all that was 'heathen', they look askance at attempts to adapt the faith to traditional culture. African clergy have been shocked to be told to abandon their clerical collars and wear decorated white gowns like Muslim leaders. Some Indian converts have burnt their Hindu scriptures, only to find that their children were studying them again. The Indian churches are slowly learning to use verses from the Vedas as a kind of Old Testament, a foundation for the New. Both leaders and church members are seeking to understand Indian wisdom as well as Greek to interpret the Gospel.

Fr Klaus Klostermaier, after spending years at a great Krishna pilgrimage-centre, wrote: 'I have not finished yet. Not for a long time. I know there are many closed gates to pass before the knowledge of Christ becomes full reality. But I believe this is the way . . . Greek christology has not exhausted the mystery of Christ, though it has helped the Church the better to see some aspects of Christ. Indian wisdom, too, will not exhaust the mystery of Christ. But it would help the Church in India to understand Christ better and to let him be really understood.'[4]

[4] *Hindu and Christian in Vrindaban*, p. 118.

INDEX